Virginia

Virginia

Jean F. Blashfield

Children's Press®
A Division of Grolier Publishing
New York London Hong Kong Sydney
Danbury, Connecticut

Frontispiece: Thornton Gap, Shenandoah National Park

Front cover: Monticello

Back cover: Blue Ridge Parkway

SwC
J
975.5
Blas

Consultant: Rita G. Koman, Virginia Historical Consultant

34.00

Please note: All statistics are as up-to-date as possible at the time of publication.

Book production by Editorial Directions, Inc.

Library of Congress Cataloging-in-Publication Data

Blashfield, Jean F.
    Virginia / Jean F. Blashfield.
       144 p. 24 cm. — (America the beautiful. Second series)
    Includes bibliographical references and indexes.
    Summary : Describes the geography, plants and animals, history, economy, language,
religions, culture, and people of the state of Virginia.
    ISBN 0-516-20831-4
    1. Virginia—Juvenile literature. [1. Virginia.] I. Title. II. Series.
F226.3.B57 1998
975.5—dc21   98-38560
                                                                                         CIP
                                                                                          AC

Acknowledgments

Like all writers, I am totally indebted to librarians. They are the people who treasure information, delight in organizing it, relish confirming it, and rejoice in sharing it. My special thanks for assistance in preparing this book go to: Arlington (Virginia) Public Library; the publications of the historical and national park sites in Virginia; the Hedburg Public Library, Janesville, Wisconsin; the University of Wisconsin—Madison Memorial Library (and their fine catalog on the Internet); the State Historical Society of Wisconsin; and to Cindy Black, whose mother's collection of books on her native Virginia has been of invaluable help.

Old Town in Alexandria

Alexandria's City Hall

Crabtree Falls

Contents

An Assateague Island pony

Virginia Beach

Mount Vernon

Clamming in the Chesapeake

Tiger swallowtail butterfly

CHAPTER ONE

Virginia Is . . .

irginia is the cornerstone of American history. The growth of the original thirteen colonies spread out from Virginia. Its position in the Middle Atlantic states makes it a transitional state, with qualities of both North and South.

Virginia is a land full of ideals. The ideals developed by Virginia's colonists are the ones that formed the Declaration of Independence and the Constitution of the United States, so the spirit of early Virginia runs through the nation and its culture.

King Charles I of England was the inspiration for Virginia's nickname, "Old Dominion."

Virginia is the state with the longest continuous recorded history. Visits to its shores were noted by explorers in the 1500s. Then, in 1607, Europeans came to stay, forming the first of the thirteen colonies.

Virginia is proud of its nicknames. The people are known as Cavaliers because they were loyal to King Charles I in the English Civil War (1642–1651). His son, Charles II, gave the colony the nickname "Old Dominion" for that same loyalty. He probably honored Virginia with the name, which meant that it was equal to

Opposite: Lewis Spring Falls

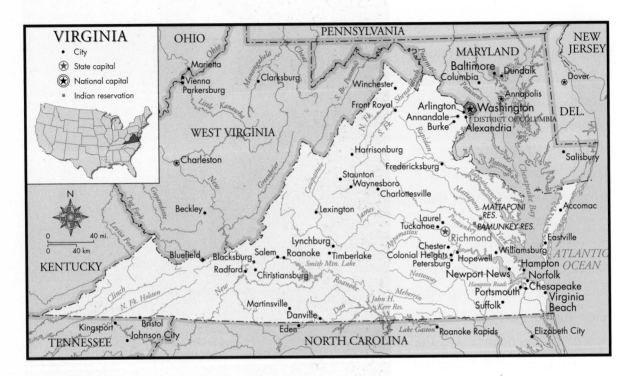

VIRGINIA
- • City
- ⭑ State capital
- ⭐ National capital
- ▪ Indian reservation

OHIO
PENNSYLVANIA
NEW JERSEY

MARYLAND
Baltimore
Columbia • • Dundalk
• Marietta
• Vienna
Parkersburg
Clarksburg •
Winchester •
• Dover
• Annapolis
WEST VIRGINIA
Front Royal •
Arlington •
Washington
Annandale •
Burke •
DISTRICT OF COLUMBIA
Alexandria •
DEL.

• Charleston
Harrisonburg •
Fredericksburg •
• Salisbury
Staunton •
Waynesboro •
Charlottesville •
N
• Accomac
MATTAPONI RES.
Beckley •
Lexington •
Laurel •
Tuckahoe •
PAMUNKEY RES.
0   40 mi.
0   40 km
Lynchburg •
Richmond ⭑
• Eastville
KENTUCKY
Chester •
Williamsburg •
ATLANTIC OCEAN
Bluefield •
Blacksburg •
Salem • Roanoke • Timberlake
Colonial Heights •
Petersburg •
Hopewell •
Hampton •
Radford •
Christiansburg •
Smith Mtn. Lake
Newport News •
Norfolk •
Chesapeake •
Portsmouth •
Virginia Beach •
Martinsville •
Suffolk •
Danville •
Kingsport •
Bristol •
Johnson City •
Eden •
Roanoke Rapids •
Elizabeth City •
TENNESSEE
NORTH CAROLINA

Geopolitical map of Virginia

England in importance. Virginia is called "Mother of Presidents" because it has produced eight of them, more than any other state.

Virginia is, according to its constitution, a commonwealth instead of a state. Only three other states in the nation use that term—Massachusetts, Kentucky, and Pennsylvania.

Virginia is a land that has seen terrible wars. The American Revolution began with protests in the colony's legislature and ended on a battlefield at Yorktown. The Civil War battles began and ended in Virginia, killing about 300,000 men within the boundaries of the state and marking its people for the next century.

Virginia is a state that treasures its tradition but is willing to change. In the 1600s and 1700s, Virginia's development took place

along the James River. The next century moved westward into the mountains. The 1900s has seen the north, along the Potomac River, grow by incredible leaps. What the fifth century, starting in 2001, will bring will surely be as fascinating as the first four.

An early scene of the Potomac River

CHAPTER TWO

A Colony, a Nation

Little did the Englishmen who came ashore from a wide Virginia river imagine that they were starting a new era in the history of the world. The events that would eventually boil up into an important new nation were beginning to simmer.

These Englishmen were not alone on the continent. The Spanish had already edged into Florida, the French and the Dutch were exploring the resources of the new land farther north, and the continent was already occupied by the people we have come to call Native Americans.

Land in northern Virginia, where the French and Dutch explored

They Were There First

Flint Run in Warren County contains the ruins of the earliest structure built in the Western Hemisphere. It has been dated as being at least 10,000 years old. But nothing is known about the people who built that structure. Over the centuries, the Native Americans moved and acquired new skills. They formed tribes and dissolved alliances.

It has been estimated that there were probably about 10,000 Native Americans in Virginia in 1607. Tribes in the region spoke languages belonging to three different language groups.

A few small groups of Siouan people lived in the Shenandoah Valley and hunted bison, but most Sioux Indians, and most

Opposite: Skyline Drive at Shenandoah National Park

Native Americans fishing on early Virginia's shores

bison, lived far to the west. The Cherokee lived in the mountains. These Iroquoian people knew a great deal about farming and tools.

Near the coast, Algonquin-speaking Indians lived in a number of small villages. Each village was led by a chief, or *werowance*. The English newcomers found that about thirty of these villages had established a loose alliance called the Powhatan Confederation. It was headed by a leader also called Powhatan, though his Indian name was probably *Wahunsonacock*. These Indians are usually referred to collectively as the Powhatan Confederation. One Powhatan tribe, the Accomac, lived across Chesapeake Bay on the peninsula now known as the Eastern Shore.

A Powhatan village usually consisted of about a hundred families living in separate wigwams. They used metal only for ornaments, and they had no domesticated animals except dogs. They hunted with bows and arrows. They grew maize, or corn, using sticks and antlers for tools.

These Native Americans also grew tobacco, which was used for both religious ceremonies and pleasure. It was tobacco that would eventually mean the survival of Virginia as a colony.

Coming to Virginia

After visiting North America in 1584, Walter Raleigh reported to Queen Elizabeth that the land he had seen around Roanoke Island was inviting. She graciously allowed the land to be called *Virginia* after her own nickname. Elizabeth was called the "Virgin Queen" because she had never married and was said to be married to her kingdom.

Other expeditions failed to establish settlements, but the English were nothing if not determined. After Queen Elizabeth's death in 1603, the new king, James I, encouraged the founding of a colony in Virginia. The adventurers who wanted to participate paid a fee and became part owners of the London Company, which then established the Virginia Company to do the actual work of colonizing Virginia.

Three ships set sail for Virginia from England on December 20, 1606. They were the *Sarah Constant* (sometimes called the *Susan*

Exploration of Virginia

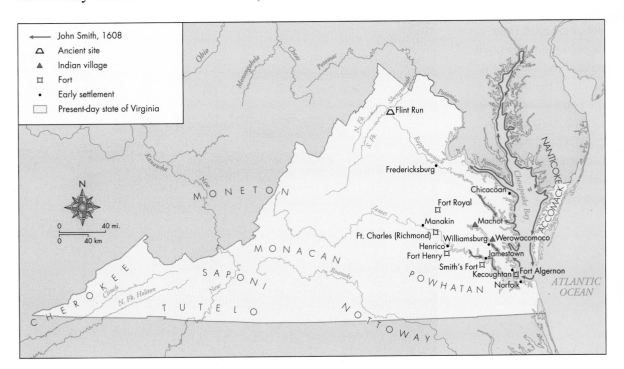

Constant), the *Goodspeed*, and the *Discovery*. Even though almost one-third of the people who sailed died on the way, the 105 adventurers were certain that the strange new world would make them wealthy and reveal a route to the fabled Orient, where even greater wealth awaited them. For many, that dream would last decades.

The ships sailed past Cape Henry into the huge natural harbor now called Hampton Roads. Sixty miles (96 km) up a river called the Powhatan on their map, they landed on May 13, 1607. People from the first boats described the river, which they called the James, as the "broade, sweete river." But, in fact, the water wasn't sweet. It was brackish, meaning that it was part saltwater and part freshwater, and the salt content made them ill.

Because it was springtime, their landing place seemed to offer

The James River

all they wanted, but as the heat of summer increased, they discovered that they had settled on a humid, swampy, insect-ridden island with no drinkable water. However, many decided to stay where they were. Some sailed their ship up the deep river until it was blocked by waterfalls and rapids. There they claimed the land in the name of the king by writing on a wooden cross they planted in the soil the words "Jacobus Rex—1607," meaning "James the King—1607."

John Smith and Trouble

The colony's first leaders were chosen by men in London who wrote down their choices and sealed the paper in a small box. Not until the adventurers arrived in Virginia were they allowed to know who had been chosen. The president was Edward Maria Wingfield. The others were all gentlemen or experienced sailors except one— John Smith. He was probably named because he had some military experience. Little did the London Council dream that the ungentlemanly Smith would save their colony.

John Smith with the Powhatans

On landing, the other men of the council were determined to start hunting for treasure immediately. But Smith insisted that they fortify their James Citie (today called Jamestown) settlement to keep it safe from attack.

When Smith lost the argument, he joined a few fortune hunters in a small boat on a jaunt up the James River. They returned to Jamestown to find that it had been attacked by Indians of the Powhatan Confederation.

BURNING OF JAMESTOWN.

One of a number of Jamestown fires that destroyed Jamestown during the seventeeth century

Several settlers were killed or injured before the guns of the ships lying at anchor could be used against the attackers.

Many of the first colonists had fun waiting for good fortune to come to them. They were, after all, "gentlemen," and gentlemen did not do manual labor. They would not even plant a crop. They assumed that their supply ship from England would arrive long before a crop could be grown, so why bother? John Smith wrote that the "gentlemen" in the party never "ceased their malice, grudging and muttering."

Reality set in as almost half of the 105 men died of unknown diseases over the summer. When the supply ship finally arrived in January 1608, only thirty-eight settlers were still alive. The houses that Smith had forced them to build had soon caught fire, leaving only three small buildings in which they packed themselves that first winter.

The London Council seriously considered calling a halt to the whole project. They voted to continue a bit longer. Late in 1608, a ship carried the first two women to Virginia. They were the wives of two colonists. The next year, the London Council sent nine more ships, though only seven arrived. On board were more women.

The Starving Time

Three hundred new settlers arrived with high hopes in August 1609. But when new ships arrived the following spring, only sixty-five settlers were still alive. There had not been enough food

The Pocahontas Story (Part One)

John Smith was only twenty-seven when he helped settle Jamestown. He had been a soldier who fought the Turks and had even been kidnapped and sold into slavery. The "gentlemen" in Virginia resented his leadership, but he kept them alive during that first summer and fall.

Smith found Indians who did not belong to the Powhatan Confederation and traded with them for food, taking care not to venture into Powhatan territory. But he wasn't careful enough. The men with him were killed, and he was taken prisoner.

Marched to a large lodge where the leaders of the confederation met, Smith was questioned about the strangers' intentions. Then, according to Smith's report, he was bound to rocks and about to be beaten to death with clubs when Powhatan's daughter, Matoaka (called *Pocahontas*, meaning "playful one"), lay across him in protection. Smith was then set free.

Some historians think that what Smith went through was more likely an adoption ceremony, in which he was found acceptable and perhaps taken into the tribe. If so, that acceptance did not protect the Jamestown colony. ■

Settlers in early Virginia lived in difficult conditions.

to last the winter, and there was nothing to plant that spring. The survivors were too weak to last out the dreaded summer sickness. They prepared to go back to England.

But before the disheartened colonists could clear the James River, they met a ship carrying more supplies, more settlers, and a new governor, Lord Delaware. He refused to let the them leave. Just when the colony might have failed, it found new heart in a governor who was determined to make Virginia prosper.

It was another man, Sir Thomas Dale—working under Lord Delaware—who really settled the colony. Previously all the land and all the supplies belonged to all the colonists equally, so there was no incentive for a lazy man to work. But Dale granted private land to those who would prepare and plant it. Suddenly, there was more food than there had been before, and the men had a reason to work hard. The colonists spread out, claiming land at a fair distance from Jamestown.

Prominent among the men determined to make the colony thrive was John Rolfe, who saw that tobacco could be important. When he found that Virginia tobacco did not please the tastes of Englishmen, he found a gentler-tasting tobacco in the Caribbean and began to plant it in Virginia. Despite the fact that King James himself had declared tobacco a "loathsome" weed, Virginians quickly discovered that the plant could be profitable. Rolfe's seeds would help save the colony.

The Death of Friendship

By 1621, the colonists had gathered enough funds to start a free school for both English and native children, so that they could grow together as friends. The school's headmaster, or principal, worked hard to increase the friendship between the Indians and the colonists. He even built an English-style house for Powhatan's brother, Opechancanough.

An English house was not enough for Opechancanough, however, who replaced Powhatan as head of the thirty Powhatan villages. He continued to appear friendly, but he secretly planned a massive attack on the settlers.

On March 22, 1622, while some Indians breakfasted with colonists, others attacked settlers at eighty different locations—all at one time. More than 350 settlers—at least one-fourth of the population—died. Tobacco planter John Rolfe died, as did the friendly principal of the Jamestown school. The deaths among the colonists would have been even greater but for the help of an Indian boy named Chanco, who had become a Christian. He told his employer, who warned the governor of Jamestown of the planned attack.

This massacre was the beginning of the end of English attempts to be friendly to the Indians. From then on, the settlers worked to keep Indians out of their area, and they moved into protective forts.

The Pocahontas Story (Part Two)

Whatever the reason Pocahontas saved John Smith, the "romance" didn't last. John Smith left for England, and the men who remained in Virginia kidnapped Pocahontas and held her captive, hoping to prevent attacks by the Powhatans. She converted to Christianity and fell in love with settler John Rolfe. In 1616, the governor of the colony sent Rolfe, Pocahontas, and their son to England to publicize the possibilities of Virginia. London society fawned over the Native American woman, but just before she was to return to Virginia, she caught smallpox and died at Gravesend, where she was buried. ■

The Advent of Slavery

The year 1619 was eventful in Virginia. A ship full of very welcome women arrived to marry lonely adventuring men. Governor Sir George Yeardley came to establish a representative government. It was to consist of an upper house of the men already on the Council of State and a lower house—called the House of Burgesses—that would include representatives from the different regions or boroughs of Virginia.

Also that year, some people arrived in Virginia who would not be represented in the government for 250 years. They were black men from Africa who had been taken as booty by a Dutch ship from a Spanish ship. The Dutch sold them in Virginia as indentured servants. After serving as unpaid servants for a certain period of time, they were to become freedmen.

Slaves being introduced into the Virginia colony

As tobacco-growing became increasingly successful, however, tobacco farmers found it hard to get cheap labor. They saw what the Spanish on the Caribbean islands had already seen—enslaving the black people was efficient. In 1661, Virginia's House of Burgesses (colonial legialature) wrote the first American law leading to slavery.

Slavery paid off in Virginia because the land was still being claimed for development. The English were delighted to discover that the black Africans appeared to be used to working in hot, muggy, mosquito-ridden places.

By 1700, when Virginia had about 70,000

Bacon's Rebellion

Some colonists disliked having decisions made for them by the men in government. In 1676, settler Nathaniel Bacon led a rebellion against the governor, Sir William Berkeley.

Bacon was furious because Berkeley had ordered that no one could attack Indians unless he personally approved. But when his own property and a friend were harmed by marauders, Bacon wanted to deal with them. Berkeley said Bacon would be labeled a rebel if he counterattacked. Angered, Bacon and his followers marched on Jamestown and its statehouse. Berkeley was forced to flee, and Bacon burned down the statehouse—and the town.

Bacon's Rebellion, as the event has been called, is regarded as a step in the development of democracy in America. But it is more likely that Bacon and his neighbors just wanted to be left alone to kill Indians to protect their property. When Bacon died of a disease soon afterward, Berkeley returned to Jamestown and executed a large number of Bacon's followers. He was later recalled to England due to the harshness of his penalties. ■

people, Africans were being brought into Virginia at the rate of about a thousand a year. As black people gradually began to outnumber whites in some communities, laws and controls were made even harsher to prevent rebellion. Even so, historians have counted at least seventy slave revolts during the following years.

Of course, some people questioned the right of one person to own another. Though they may not have taken action against slavery at the time, they did their best to make their slaves comfortable. Thomas Jefferson, for example, housed his slaves in brick houses, with well-made doors and windows that kept out the cold and rain, and with wooden floors. He gave them good clothing and dealt with them directly instead of hiring an overseer to take charge.

Unlike Jefferson, though, most upper-class Virginians did not even question their right to own slaves. The matter would come to a head in the mid-1800s.

Opening Up Virginia

Englishmen and Africans were not the only newcomers to Virginia. French Huguenots began to arrive about 1660, and continued to do so for many decades. These were French people who, unlike most of their fellow citizens, were not Catholic. They were forced to leave France, and many of them settled in Virginia, at Manakin, the first settlement built above the Fall Line on the James River.

In the 1730s, the Crown opened up the Valley of Virginia to settlement, encouraging German and Scotch-Irish immigrants from Pennsylvania to move southward. These people, used to being independent in their homelands, spurned slavery.

As newcomers to Virginia moved westward, they ran into land claimed by the French, who had come southward from Canada and claimed the entire Mississippi Valley, including the Ohio River Valley in the Allegheny Mountains. Starting in 1754, this conflict became the French and Indian War, which was part of a larger, European struggle called the Seven Years' War. In the American colonies, the war resulted in France giving up all rights to land east of the Mississippi River. Those Virginians who had moved westward now had every right to be there.

The French and Indian War

Giving Up "Home"

England's attitude toward its colonies in North America was that they existed only to provide a growing economic base for the mother country. The colonists, however,

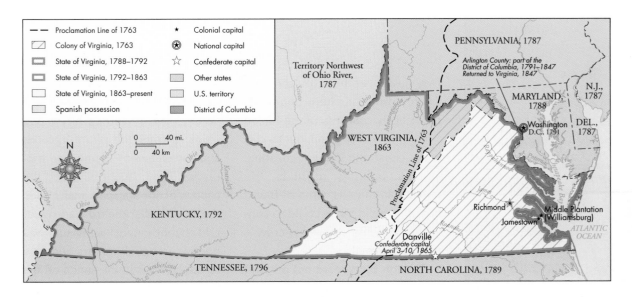

Legend:
- – – Proclamation Line of 1763
- Colony of Virginia, 1763
- State of Virginia, 1788–1792
- State of Virginia, 1792–1863
- State of Virginia, 1863–present
- Spanish possession
- ★ Colonial capital
- National capital
- ☆ Confederate capital
- Other states
- U.S. territory
- District of Columbia

N

0   40 mi.
0   40 km

Territory Northwest
of Ohio River,
1787

PENNSYLVANIA, 1787

Arlington County: part of the
District of Columbia, 1791–1847
Returned to Virginia, 1847

N.J.,
1787

MARYLAND,
1788

DEL.,
1787

Washington
D.C., 1791

WEST VIRGINIA,
1863

KENTUCKY, 1792

Richmond

Middle Plantation
(Williamsburg)

Jamestown

ATLANTIC
OCEAN

Danville
Confederate capital,
April 3–10, 1865

TENNESSEE, 1796

NORTH CAROLINA, 1789

Historical map of Virginia

came to believe that the colonies existed for the rights of the people who lived there.

In the mid-1700s, England's policies began to harm the colony's growth instead of encourage it. First, Parliament (the English legislature) began to outlaw the production in America of finished goods that could be sold abroad. They allowed only raw materials to be shipped out of the colony. Then, they insisted that items shipped from Virginia had to travel on British ships. Finally, Parliament passed laws requiring the colonies to pay new taxes that would pay for the Seven Years' War. For the first time, Virginians wondered if they really were still English.

In 1765, Parliament passed the Stamp Act, a law requiring a tax stamp on every document or newspaper published in the colony. Patrick Henry, representing Hanover County, spoke out against it. He proposed that only the Virginia legislature could tax Virginians. Later, Henry urged Virginians to take up arms against the British with these words: "I know not what course others may take, but, as for me, give me liberty, or give me death!"

The Prince of Villains

Edward Teach, called Blackbeard, may have been born in Accomack County on the Eastern Shore. It's more likely that this pirate hailed from Bristol in England, but he certainly chose the Virginia coastline as his hunting grounds. He rejoiced in the nickname of Blackbeard, and did all he could to convince everyone—even his crew—that he was evil.

Though Blackbeard hid out and lived primarily in North Carolina, Alexander Spotswood, governor of Virginia from 1710 to 1722, was determined to crush piracy in the colony. The governor hired two ships to track the pirate into the shallow waters of sounds and tributaries. They caught him, and the captain of one ship personally killed the pirate. Blackbeard had never told anyone where his treasure was buried, and avid hunters continue to search for it in the sands off the East Coast. ■

Other colonies heard about Henry's words and the passage of his resolution. They petitioned the king to cancel the Stamp Act. Parliament did repeal it, but they weren't through imposing taxes.

Massachusetts leaders reacted to a new tax on tea by dumping tea into the harbor at Boston. When Virginia's House of Burgesses demonstrated support for the move, the governor, Lord Dunmore, dissolved the legislative body. The Burgesses continued to meet illegally and arranged with Massachusetts and other colonies to create a Continental Congress that would unite the colonies against the British government.

Patrick Henry

Taking Action

Meeting in Philadelphia on September 5, 1774, the representatives to the Continental Congress chose a Virginian, Peyton Randolph, to lead them. They resolved to oppose the British policy, but little else happened until 1775, when British troops fired on Americans at Lexington and Concord in Massachusetts. Armed warfare seemed inevitable.

A second Continental Congress met and chose George Washington of Virginia as the commander-in-chief of whatever army it assembled. The Congress also formed an informal government to take charge of the thirteen colonies during a struggle against the Crown. Only gradually did the Congress realize that the colonies would have to declare complete independence if they were to survive as free people. Virginia delegate Thomas Jefferson, who had not been part of the first meeting, wrote, in very simple form, a Declaration of Independence.

The War in Virginia

The army that had trained George Washington now found itself facing him in battle. Those battles took place mainly in the northern colonies, but Virginia contributed men, money, and weapons. In addition to Washington, other Virginians served as well. Scottish-born John Paul Jones, who lived in Fredericksburg, started the U. S. Navy. George Rogers Clark, a native of Albemarle County, claimed the Northwest Territory for the patriots. Because of his military prowess, the new United States would later have states in the Ohio River Valley.

The British Army did not approach Virginia until 1780, when they came in through the mountain region and the Carolinas. The mountain people refused to join the British, and soon a full-scale invasion of Virginia was underway. It was led by Benedict Arnold and Lord Charles Cornwallis.

Lord Cornwallis was determined to destroy the Continental

Creating a Pattern for the United States

On May 15, 1776, Edmund Pendleton offered the Virginia House of Burgesses a resolution calling for independence of the colonies. In fact, Virginia declared itself a free and independent state. A few weeks later, on July 4, the same idea was approved on a larger stage, at the Continental Congress meeting in Philadelphia.

At that May House of Burgesses session, George Mason (left) of Gunston Hall in Fairfax County offered the Virginia Declaration of Rights. It declared that "all men are by nature equally free and independent and have certain inherent rights." These rights later served as the model for the Bill of Rights added to the U.S. Constitution.

In one way, George Mason failed. He bitterly opposed slavery and desperately wanted it to be outlawed in the Constitution, but he failed to convince all the other southerners. ■

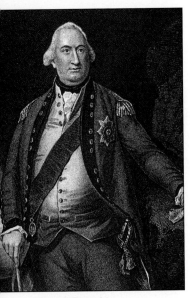

Lord Charles Cornwallis

Army that was fighting under twenty-three-year-old French volunteer Marquis de Lafayette. But when Lafayette's troops were joined by those under General Anthony Wayne, Cornwallis gave up and headed toward Jamestown and Portsmouth, planning to meet the British Navy. Instead, Cornwallis faced a French fleet, led by Admiral François-Joseph-Paul de Grasse, who was on the side of the Americans.

Cornwallis debated turning inland away from the navy, but George Washington's troops sneaked up behind him, trapping him near Yorktown. On October 19, 1781, Lord Cornwallis surrendered to American and French forces while a military band played "The World Turned Upside Down."

During the war, political leaders in Virginia and the Continental Congress were busy forming a state and a nation. At first, they formed a loose confederation of states, but it soon became clear that such loosely joined states could not form a nation. They wrote a new Constitution to govern a more closely knit group of states.

A Traitor in Virginia

Benedict Arnold was an American whose name came to mean "traitor." He had served as a loyal officer of the Continental Army until he was passed over for promotion. Angered, he secretly joined the royalist cause. In 1780, he led the British through Virginia, determined to take the new capital of Richmond. He managed to destroy most of the city before the Virginia militia drove out his army.

In January 1781, Arnold's destination was Westham, where guns were made for the Continental Army. But some Virginians dumped the guns in the James River. Arnold found the factory and town empty.

When the Redcoats pulled out, the Virginians returned and quickly rebuilt so that they could continue to make arms for their troops.

Not all Virginians were in favor of independence, however. The illustrious Byrd family, for example, welcomed Benedict Arnold into their home. But even the royalists turned against Arnold when he betrayed a British spy, John André, to the Americans and André was hanged. Benedict Arnold escaped to England, where he lived out his life condemned by all sides. ■

As each state approved, or ratified, the Constitution, it was taken into the new United States of America. Virginia became the tenth state admitted, on June 25, 1788. Virginia's George Washington became the first president of the United States.

The "Father of Our Country"

George Washington was a plantation owner and soldier who had fought in the French and Indian War. He knew Virginia well because he had also worked as a surveyor, studying and measuring the land of the colony. The Continental Congress knew that he was a patriot, experienced, and willing to serve without pay as commander of the troops.

There were many times during the war with the British when the colonists might have failed, but Washington's determination kept the Continental Army fighting. That same determination to make the new country succeed got him elected to two terms as the first president of the United States, serving from 1789 to 1797. ■

CHAPTER THREE

A Century of Growth, Change, and War

irginia began its statehood as a central part of the new nation.
It gave up a triangle of its land on the Potomac River to help
form the capital of the nation, the District of Columbia, which
came to be called Washington after Virginia's hero. The state's
leaders who had played such an important role in its formation
became the leaders of that new nation. Four of the first five presidents were Virginians. Only John Adams, the second president, was
from Massachusetts.

One of the most important steps Virginia's General Assembly
took in the early years was to pass Thomas Jefferson's Statute for
Religious Liberty. In it, Virginia completely separated the church
from the state. No longer would a person have to be a Protestant to
hold public office. Nor could public money be used to support a
specific religion. This principle was adopted by the nation as the
First Amendment to the Constitution.

Opposite: A slave's
house on a Virginia
plantation

Twenty-Five Years of Virginia Presidents

For the first twenty-five years of the nineteenth century, the presidency of the United States belonged to three Virginians. Two had been governors of the state. Two had served in the U.S. Congress, and all three had played an influential role in the founding of the nation.

Thomas Jefferson (above left), the third president, served from 1801 to 1809. The author of the Declaration of Independence, he made the huge Louisiana Purchase that doubled the size of the United States. However, he later said that he was proudest of having founded the University of Virginia in Charlottesville. He designed most of that university as well as his own home, Monticello. Jefferson was born at Shadwell, in Albemarle County.

James Madison (below left), the fourth president, served from 1809 to 1817. He played a leading role in writing the U.S. Constitution, sponsored the Bill of Rights, and was secretary of state under Jefferson. A native of Port Conway, he retired from the presidency to his plantation, Montpelier, near the Blue Ridge Mountains.

James Monroe (above), the fifth president, served from 1817 to 1825. Born in Westmoreland County, he studied law under Jefferson while that future president was governor of the state. Jefferson made Monroe minister to France to help negotiate the Louisiana Purchase. As president, Monroe formed permanent U.S. foreign policy with the Monroe Doctrine, which warned European nations to stay out of the Western Hemisphere. ■

Virginian John Marshall, who was Thomas Jefferson's cousin, became chief justice of the U.S. Supreme Court in 1801. During the thirty-four years he served in that position, he established the court's right to make decisions interpreting the Constitution. That right has been the backbone of the American judicial system ever since.

War Again

In 1811, a new war with Britain seemed to be gathering momentum. It was basically part of the huge Napoleonic Wars in Europe. In the United States, it grew out of the British Navy's kidnapping American sailors and forcing them to serve on British ships. British ships even fired on several American ships off the Virginia coast. In addition, Britain was keeping the United States from trading with France.

The Virginia General Assembly voted in favor of war in January 1812, but it was another five months before the U.S. Congress agreed. For two years, Virginians suffered invasions along their coasts and rivers, especially around Norfolk, which the British hoped to capture. In what came to be called the Battle of Craney Island, the American defenders succeeded in preventing England from taking their huge harbor. The British retaliated by burning the city of Hampton. Then, in 1814, the British burned the capital city of Washington, across the Potomac from Virginia, and briefly captured and held the city of Alexandria. An agreement was reached between the two nations before more damage was done.

Virginians Go West

In 1803, President Jefferson purchased from France the huge central part of what is now the United States, for less than 3 cents an acre (1.2 cents ha). But no one in the eastern states knew much about the incredible Louisiana Purchase. Jefferson sent Meriwether Lewis and William Clark to explore the new land. Both men were Virginia natives. They spent three years on the trek from St. Louis, Missouri, to the Pacific Ocean and back again. ■

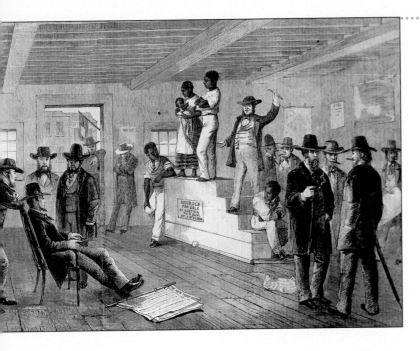

A slave auction in Virginia

The Call to Free the Slaves

Virginia began the nineteenth century with more slaves than any other state. But not all Virginians were in favor of slavery. Such men as George Washington, Patrick Henry, George Mason, and John Randolph tried to figure out ways to abolish, or get rid of, slavery in the United States.

Many plantation owners freed their own slaves, either gradually over the years or on the owners' deaths. This led to a population of about 50,000 free black people living in the state in the years before the Civil War (1861–1865). Other slave owners were willing to free their slaves, but they wanted to be paid for them. Virginia did pay to send some former slaves to the new colony of Liberia in Africa, which was founded in 1821 by the American Colonization Society. Only a few thousand freed slaves were ever transported to Africa, but probably half of them were from Virginia.

Though such efforts by individuals and organizations were good for antislavery, most plantation owners in eastern Virginia regarded slaves as vital to their financial success. It was evident as early as 1830 that votes on slavery in the General Assembly divided the western part of the state and the eastern, or Tidewater, region. In one vote, the abolition of slavery came within seven votes of

Nat Turner

Nat Turner was born into slavery in 1800 in Southampton County. As a young man, he became certain that he was appointed by God to lead his people out of slavery. He planned to kill all white people and establish a black nation in Virginia.

Starting on August 21, 1831, Turner and his followers went from house to house, killing about sixty people. Two days later, the rebellious slaves reached the home of Dr. Samuel Blunt. Blunt, having been warned of the uprising, gave his own slaves the choice of defending their plantation, Belmont, or joining Nat Turner. Blunt's slaves chose to fight for Blunt and Belmont. As Turner and his greatly reduced group of followers neared Belmont, they were ambushed and defeated. Eventually, twenty of the rebels were executed. Turner himself was hanged in November, after dictating his own account of the insurrection to his attorney. ■

passing. If there had been money in the treasury to pay for the loss of the slaves, the vote probably would have passed.

Instead of abolishing slavery, Virginians found themselves tightening the controls on their slaves. They resented the way that

The Virginia Decade—Presidents 9, 10, and 12

Three more Virginians were president of the United States starting in 1841. William Henry Harrison (below), born in Virginia but living in Ohio, was elected. His vice president, John Tyler (right), was also from Virginia. Both of them were born in Charles City County. Harrison had won fame as an Indian fighter and was the victor in the Battle of Tippecanoe in 1811. He commanded American troops in the War of 1812

(1812–1815). Harrison caught a cold during his inauguration in March 1841 as the ninth president. He died thirty days later. His presidency is the shortest in U.S. history.

Tyler then became the tenth president, the first vice president to move up to that position. He had been the governor of Virginia, as had his father. Tyler's presidency lasted until 1845. During his term, he tried to prevent the rights of states from being taken over by the federal government.

Tyler chose not to run again and the presidency was taken over by James K. Polk of North Carolina and Tennessee. He was president during the war with Mexico, which left Texas and California in the hands of the United States. But before the decade was out, Zachary Taylor (below), a native of Orange County, was elected to be the twelfth president. A soldier, he had gained fame as a hero of the Mexican War. ■

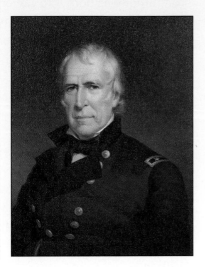

abolitionists from the North interfered in their lives. And they feared that rebellions like Nat Turner's might lead to more deaths.

The General Assembly passed laws that made the lives of slaves harsher than ever. Even freedmen found their movements restricted because white people refused to trust them. The lives of so-called "free" African-Americans were not really free. They were governed by laws that kept them from owning firearms, staying out late at night, or even learning to read and write. And after Nat Turner's Rebellion, black people were even prohibited from becoming ministers.

The Mexican War of the 1840s resulted in new territory for the United States. Southerners began to fear that more new states would be admitted to the union as non-slave states, leaving them greatly outnumbered in Congress. Virginia-born representative Henry Clay played an important role in delaying war between the North and South with several compromises. The North gave in on some decisions, while the South gave in on others, but the compromises didn't work.

Anger over slavery built up, fed by the publication in 1852 of Harriet Beecher Stowe's novel *Uncle Tom's Cabin.* It gave a painful and dramatic picture of life in slavery. In 1854, Margaret Douglass of Norfolk was sent to jail for a month because she opened a school for free black children.

In October 1859, Northern abolitionist John Brown raided the U. S. Arsenal at Harper's Ferry, Virginia (in an area that would soon become West Virginia). He and his followers were planning to arm the slaves and lead an insurrection. Instead, he was caught and hanged. But it was clear that deadly events were about to happen.

Secession

The idea for Virginia to secede, or withdraw, from the Union was not a new idea. Virginians and other Southerners had been think-

Robert E. Lee, Virginian and National Hero

Anne Carter of Shirley Plantation married "Light Horse" Harry Lee, who had gained fame during the American Revolution. Their children, one of whom was Robert Edward, were born at Stafford, the Lee plantation in Westmoreland County. Robert was raised in Alexandria and went to the U.S. Military Academy at West Point. He married Mary, the only daughter of George Washington Parke Custis and later became the owner of Custis's estate in Arlington. Lee was with the U.S. Army in Texas when the Civil War started and President Lincoln asked him to head the Union forces. But even though he opposed slavery, Lee chose to fight for Virginia instead of the United States. And it was in Virginia that, four years later, General Lee was forced to surrender to General Ulysses S. Grant.

After the Confederacy's defeat in 1865, Lee became president of Washington College at Lexington. It was later renamed Washington and Lee University. ■

ing about the possibility of secession for many years over issues other than slavery. Northerners controlled the U.S. Congress, and the South thought that many bills Congress passed benefited only the North. They also thought that Congress often took away

Virginia's right to organize its own affairs. They felt their rights under the Constitution were slipping away.

In December 1860, South Carolina made the first call for secession. Several other states followed, but Virginia was slow to join in the move to form a new Confederate States of America. The state that had nurtured the new United States was reluctant to help destroy it.

It wasn't until President Abraham Lincoln wanted Virginia to supply troops to fight the seceding states that Virginians voted to join the Confederacy. The capital of the new Confederate States was moved from Montgomery, Alabama, to Richmond. In Virginia, as elsewhere in the South, the war that followed is often referred to as the War for Southern Independence.

Losing Fifty Counties

As early as 1816, Virginians in the western part of the state asked for a change in the state constitution that would allow people who didn't own land to vote. They also wanted to be able to vote for their own county officials instead of accepting people appointed by the governor. Gradually, slavery, too, became an issue separating the people in the western part of the state from the more tradition-minded people in the eastern Tidewater area.

In 1861, the mountain men chose to ignore the convention at which other Virginians voted to secede from the Union. Instead, the leaders of the fifty counties in the northwestern part of the state went to Washington and asked permission to form a new state—West Virginia. Statehood was granted in 1863. Overnight, Virginia lost 35 percent of its land and 25 percent of its people.

The War Years

For four years, the Civil War was fought to a large extent on Virginia soil. The first major battle took place in Virginia on July 21, 1861. It is called the First Battle of Bull Run by the North (which named battles after rivers and streams) and the First Battle of Manassas by the South (which named battles after towns). This battle was won by the South, giving the Confederates confidence that they could whip the Union.

In June 1862, Robert E. Lee, a former Union Army officer, was placed in command of the Confederate Army of Northern Virginia. He proceeded to defeat Union troops in many battles in Virginia, until he decided to move northward into Pennsylvania, the North's own territory. There, at Gettysburg, he suffered a severe defeat. He was forced to take his forces back into Virginia, where he concentrated on protecting Richmond from General Ulysses S. Grant's army.

It took two more years and hundreds of major battles and minor skirmishes on Virginia soil before the South accepted defeat. The greater number and better equipment of Union soldiers took their toll.

No other patch of land was more fought over than the area between the Potomac and the James Rivers in Virginia. The city of Winchester changed hands at least seventy times during the war. The residents never knew from one week to the next which side held their fate.

A last major battle of the Civil War also took place on Virginia soil. The Union had been held at Petersburg, near Richmond, for months. On April 2, 1865, Robert E. Lee told the people of Rich-

A New Kind of Warfare

In the huge harbor of Hampton Roads, the Confederates salvaged a burned Union ship called the *Merrimack* and turned it into a new kind of ship. They covered its hull with iron and mounted new cannon on the ship. They also gave it a new name, the *Virginia,* but it has always been called by its earlier name in modern history—the *Merrimack.*

The Union, too, experimented with ironclad ships by building the *Monitor.* It arrived from its New York shipyard on March 8, 1862, just as the *Merrimack* destroyed several wooden warships off Newport News. The next morning, the two ironclad ships fought in the world's first such battle. Cannonballs just bounced off of each ship. Finally, a shot from the *Merrimack* hit the gun turret of the *Monitor,* and the Union ship withdrew. Two months later, the Union took Norfolk, and the Confederates had no choice but to sink the *Merrimack.* ■

mond that his troops were too weak; he could no longer defend them from the besieging Northerners. But the city the Union took had been turned into charred ruins.

On April 9, Lee surrendered to General Grant at Virginia's Appomattox Court House. Confederate president Jefferson Davis

The Terrible Pit

The Crater is a 170-foot (52-m)-long pit created by a powerful explosion that occurred—as planned—during the Civil War. Union troops had unsuccessfully besieged Confederate forces, who were blocking their way to Richmond, for several weeks in June and July of 1864. Union soldiers who were miners in civilian life offered to dig a tunnel under the Confederate lines and blow them up with gunpowder.

In great secrecy, a 510-foot (155-m) tunnel was dug, and four tons of gunpowder were carried in and ignited.

The lethal surprise worked, but only briefly. Southern soldiers quickly closed up the gap in their lines. Fighting began anew deep inside the new Crater. The Battle of the Crater was one of the largest engagements in which African-American troops took part. More than a thousand black Union soldiers were killed. The Crater is now visible at Petersburg National Military Park. ■

fled from Richmond but was captured in Georgia weeks later. He was held for two years, with the Union contemplating charging him with treason, but he was never tried. Jefferson Davis died in New Orleans in 1889, and was buried there, but four years later, his body was returned to Richmond.

The "Siren of the Shenandoah"

A resident of Martinsburg and Front Royal, Belle Boyd was nineteen years old when she killed a soldier trying to break into her mother's house to force her to raise a Union flag. She is remembered now as a heroine, but at the time, Virginians were scandalized. Boyd was acquitted, leaving her free to try to acquire Union information and get it to the Confederate troops.

She was probably truly successful as a spy only once—when she let Stonewall Jackson know about Union plans at Front Royal. But the young woman continued to spy whenever possible and was sent to prison several times for her efforts. Newspapers, especially, in the North, delighted in writing about her, and after the war, Belle Boyd built a career as a lecturer on her brief time as a Confederate spy. ■

Devastation

The Civil War devastated Virginia. First, a large portion of the state broke away as West Virginia. Second, so much of the land was fought over so often that few buildings remained standing. Third, its entire economy had been based on slavery, so with slavery gone, the people had to start from scratch to build a whole new economy. All the money they had was worthless Confederate dollars.

Day by day, step by step, Virginians had to find a new way to live. This was not an easy process. The state was deeply in debt, because when West Virginia broke away, it didn't take any of that debt with it. Instead, the new, smaller Virginia was faced with trying to pay it all.

While other states were growing and benefiting from the immigration of people from all over Europe, few of them came to Virginia, because it was well known that the state had terrible problems. In fact, many Virginians gave up their home state and headed west. Many farms were abandoned and soon reclaimed by forest, as if the last two centuries had never happened.

Virginia in ruins after
the American Civil War

Reconstruction

For several years, North-controlled Republican governments ran
the Southern states. They were determined to "reconstruct" the
South by joining important white people and former slaves in
building equal rights for everyone. But the plan failed—and it
probably would not have worked unless the North poured in great
amounts of money and people to make it succeed. Most Northerners did not want to do that, and the South didn't want the Northerners there anyway.

Those African-Americans who wanted help in finding new
ways to live beyond slavery were helped by Freedman's Bureaus set
up by the federal government throughout the South. But just as
many were harmed by promises that the bureau agents—all North-

erners—had little intention of keeping. Many African-Americans were voted into public office.

So many white people lived in poverty that they turned on African-Americans as responsible for their plight. Determined to keep black people "in their place," southern states—including Virginia—passed laws limiting their possibilities. In 1869, there were twenty-seven African-Americans in Virginia's General Assembly. When federal troops withdrew in 1876, however, black people lost all power. Virginians elected a conservative government that opposed Reconstruction. It began to pass laws that kept freed slaves from holding public office and even from voting.

Virginia was not readmitted to the Union for five years after the end of the Civil War. In the meantime, the state was run as a military district. Not even individual towns could make decisions without military approval. The U.S. government forced a new constitution on Virginians, and finally, on January 26, 1870, the state was readmitted to the Union.

The white people who had owned plantations had to find new ways to run their traditional businesses without slave labor. For most, it did not work. The children of plantation owners had to leave their farms and find work elsewhere, usually in cities. As the owners died, most of the big plantations were broken up. An era had indeed ended.

The First Black Office Holder

John Mercer Langston, a native of Louisa County, is believed to have been the first African-American elected to public office in the United States. His father (who was his mother's master) gave him his freedom when he was a child. He grew up in Ohio and attended Oberlin College, the first college to admit black students. As a young man, he was elected as the clerk in a township in Ohio. He later returned to Virginia to live and was elected to the U.S. House of Representatives in the 1890s. ■

CHAPTER FOUR

The Twentieth Century

As the twentieth century was beginning, Virginia and the whole South were still suffering from the Civil War, even though it had ended thirty-five years before. In many ways, the political leaders of the North were still punishing the South for the war by keeping it isolated from national decisions. But it was also taking a long time for the people of the South to begin to change their ideas and work for economic progress.

The issue of race relations remained a primary factor in Virginia's life. As late as 1906, one southern author wrote that the northerners who spoke against the segregation of black people "had no realization of the effect of their words upon Southern households where inmates lay down at night trembling lest they wake in flames or with black men shooting or knifing them." With that attitude, fed by wild rumors, it isn't any wonder that black versus white remained such a prominent matter in southern life.

Like other southern states, Virginia passed laws decreeing just who was a Negro, as all African-Americans were called. After the Civil War, a Negro was any person with at least one-fourth Negro blood. In 1910, that was changed to one-sixteenth. And in 1930, anyone with any black ancestry whatsoever was regarded as a Negro.

The attitudes of the South reflected in a 1904 newspaper

Opposite: NASA's Langley Research Center

Jim Crow Laws

Late in the 1800s, various southern states began to pass laws requiring African-Americans to ride in separate railway cars from white people. Virginia was the last southern state to pass such a law. Laws requiring segregation of the races were jokingly called "Jim Crow laws" after a stereotyped black man in a song-and-dance act. But they were no joke to black people. Between about 1910 and the 1930s, Virginia expanded the Jim Crow segregation from railway and bus waiting rooms to restaurants, schools, and theaters. In fact, the Jim Crow laws affected every place that people could gather. Many such laws remained in effect until the 1960s, when federal civil rights legislation was passed. ▪

Wars Bring Change

Things began to change with the election of Woodrow Wilson as president of the United States in 1912. For the first time, the southern states as a whole voted for the winner. Wilson was Virginia born, but he had lived in the North since becoming an adult, and he was governor of New Jersey when he ran for president. At least half

The Eighth President from Virginia

Thomas Woodrow Wilson, the son of a minister, was born at Staunton in 1856 but was raised in Georgia and South Carolina. He later returned to Virginia to study law, but then turned to the study of government. His ideas while teaching at Princeton University caught the attention of the public and the Democratic Party, and he was elected governor of New Jersey. In 1912, he was elected president of the United States.

Wilson tried to keep the United States neutral as World War I (1914–1918) was brewing and was reelected in 1916 on a slogan saying that he kept the United States out of the war. But as Germany sank more and more unarmed U.S. ships, he was finally forced to ask Congress to declare war on April 2, 1917. He was just as determined after the war to get the United States to join the League of Nations (the forerunner of the United Nations) but he failed, to his great disappointment. ■

of the men Wilson put in his Cabinet were from the South. Some people called the change the "end of Reconstruction."

In Virginia, as in other southern states, World War I brought a major change—but not for the good of the state. Huge numbers of African-Americans left the state to go north, where wartime industry was growing rapidly.

After the war, during the Great Depression of the 1930s, Virginia suffered along with the rest of the country. Federal projects on Virginia soil, however, changed the look of the state. For example, Skyline Drive was built, opening up Shenandoah National Park to the public.

As World War II (1939–1945) brought thousands of new residents to the Washington, D.C., area to work for the federal government, many of them moved to northern Virginia. During this time, the Pentagon was built, and Norfolk started to become a major shipbuilding and naval center. The region began to take on characteristics of northern cities, and the state split into two quite different sections. Sectionalism again played a role in Virginia politics. This time it was northern Virginia against the rest of the state.

Rapid Change

Like much of the South, Virginia reacted against the 1954 Supreme Court decision that called for desegregation of the public schools. Many white families kept their children out of school for years and put them in private academies. Some counties shut down public schools entirely, eliminating education for black children. It took several years—and more court orders—before white children and black children began to go to school together.

Blood and Race

Charles Richard Drew, an African-American physician, was fascinated by blood research. As World War II was approaching, Dr. Drew established the blood collection procedures that were used for storing blood plasma (the liquid part) for use on wounded soldiers. Because of his work, people injured at the December 1941 bombing of Pearl Harbor, which brought the United States into the war, received blood transfusions.

Unfortunately, government policy decreed that blood from white Americans had to be kept separately from blood from black Americans. Dr. Drew resigned from his job as director of the U.S. and British blood-plasma programs over that policy. He turned to other activities—especially helping African-American medical students find positions in hospitals that had long accepted only whites. He was killed in a car accident in 1950. ■

Another Supreme Court decision in 1966 called Virginia's tax on voters unconstitutional. For almost a hundred years southern states had used this tax on voters to prevent African-Americans, many of whom were too poor to pay the tax, from voting. The 1966 decision made such a tax illegal in all states, and black people began to vote in larger numbers than ever before.

Within twenty-five years, Virginians elected an African-American as governor of the state. L. Douglas Wilder, a civil rights leader, was elected in 1989. He had previously been lieutenant governor, the first black person to hold that position in a southern state. He then became the first black governor of any U.S. state.

Current Issues

Race relations in Virginia continue to be prickly. Virginia is one of the southern states in which African-American churches were burned in the 1990s. However, many thousands of African-Americans are now federal employees in northern Virginia and elsewhere. They have joined the middle classes, socially and economically.

Virginia was one of the few states that charges its citizens personal property taxes on cars. This tax had to be paid each year. A growing number of Virginians worked to have that tax repealed. With the election of Governor James Gilmore in 1997, the tax was being phased out in the late 1990s.

Since the end of the cold war with the former Soviet Union (made up of Russia and other nations), the United States has gradually been closing its military bases all over the country. Some of the many bases in Virginia have been closed, forcing the

Norfolk Naval Base

communities to find new uses for their land and new employment for their people. The Norfolk Naval Base, however, will probably continue to be vital in the twenty-first century.

Northern Virginia is now part of the huge mostly unbroken *megalopolis,* or "giant city," that stretches from Virginia north to Boston. Frequently referred to as Bos-Wash, the megalopolis is still growing. Its tentacles now reach farther and farther south and west in Virginia, gathering distant towns into the suburbs.

While Virginia's cities have grown, rural areas have continued to suffer economically. Much of the mountainous western part of Virginia is still quite undeveloped, though often the old-timers don't seem to realize it. They thrive on their independence, but are now looking toward economic equity with the rest of the state. Tourism, the state's number two industry, is helping.

Change is rapid in Virginia today. Many people are trying to hold onto the traditions that have made Virginians proud for almost four centuries. But they also know that Virginia is well situated to play an important role in the future of the United States, just as it played an important and basic role in the nation's founding.

CHAPTER FIVE

Rivers, Gaps, and Capes

A section of Virginia's long shoreline

Virginia is shaped like an elongated triangle. Because much of its east coast is on the Atlantic Ocean, it is usually called a Middle Atlantic state. It is bordered on the east and north by Washington, D.C., and Maryland, on the west by West Virginia, and on the south by North Carolina. The tip of that elongated triangle is in the southwest, where Virginia reaches between Kentucky and Tennessee. A traveler following the southern border of Virginia can go west for 440 miles (708 km) before running out of Virginia territory. That's almost as far west as the Indiana border. Perhaps Virginia shouldn't be called an eastern state at all.

Among the fifty states, Virginia is thirty-fifth in total area, with 42,326 square miles (109,625 sq. km). Its highest point is Mount Rogers, with an altitude of 5,729 feet (1,746 m), and the lowest is at sea level along the coast.

The Tidewater

Virginia has only 112 miles (180 km) of actual ocean coastline, primarily on the outer coast of the Eastern Shore. But it has 3,315 miles (5,335 km) of shoreline. This abundance of shore is due to its big rivers.

Opposite: Lake Gaston

Eastern Virginia, called the Tidewater, is divided into several peninsulas created by major rivers. Ocean water moves into those rivers in tides, which is why the region is called the Tidewater. It is also called the Coastal Plain. The region of a river in which salty ocean water mixes with freshwater from upstream is called an estuary.

Virginia's coastline consists of peninsulas alternating with the estuaries, which are part of Chesapeake Bay, one of the largest bays in the world. On the ocean side of the bay, the narrow peninsula enclosing the bay is called the Delmarva Peninsula because it forms parts of the three states of Delaware, Maryland, and Virginia. It is commonly called the Eastern Shore.

On the mainland, moving south from the Potomac River, the first peninsula is called Northern Neck. It lies between the Potomac and the Rappahannock Rivers. The Middle Peninsula lies between the Rappahannock and the York Rivers. South of that, reaching down to the James River, is the Lower Peninsula.

The coast of Virginia has many beautiful beaches and craggy projections, called capes, that jut out into the sea. But it also has gentle riverbanks in the estuaries of the wide rivers.

The Great Dismal Swamp

Because the Tidewater is so low and flat, much of the land is swampy. South of Norfolk lies the Great Dismal Swamp, which extends into North Carolina. This heavily forested swamp covers about 750 square miles (1,942 sq km). It was larger when settlers first came to the area, but parts of it have been drained for agriculture. A freshwater lake, called Lake Drummond, lies in the middle of the Dismal Swamp. A writer in 1670 described the Great Dismal Swamp as harboring "Tiggers, Bears, and other Devouring Creatures." ■

The Great Port

The most southern of the great Virginia rivers, the James, plus two smaller rivers—the Elizabeth and the Nansemond— open into a huge estuary or bay called Hampton Roads. This use of the old term "road" is short for "roadsted," meaning a place where ships lie at anchor but are not in a sheltered harbor.

The port in Norfolk

Together, the cities that lie on Hampton Roads make up one of the great ports of the United States. They include Hampton, Newport News, Portsmouth, and Norfolk. Today, bridges connect these cities. But they developed in colonial times as separate cities because they could be reached only by boat. Just beyond Norfolk is Virginia Beach, a huge resort region, and jutting out from that, on the Atlantic Ocean, is Cape Henry.

The Piedmont

Away from the coast, an abrupt change in the land occurs in an almost straight north-to-south line. This is the Fall Line, a ridge of hard rock that is higher than the Tidewater. The hard rock causes the rivers that form in the western mountains to cascade dramatically over waterfalls and rapids. Major cities—including Alexandria, Fredericksburg, and Richmond—developed along the Fall Line because it was as far as ships could go. Anything carried beyond that had to go by canoe or by land. In addition, the water-

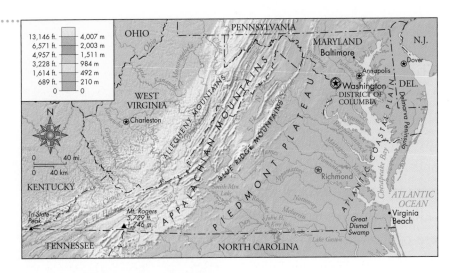

Virginia's topography

falls of the Fall Line could be used to power sawmills and flour mills. The Fall Line in Virginia is actually part of a huge Fall Line that runs from New York state down into the Deep South.

The Fall Line is the eastern boundary of the Piedmont region. *Piedmont* means "foot of the mountain" in French. It is gradually rising land that leads to the Blue Ridge Mountains and other ranges in the Appalachian Mountain system. At the Fall Line, the Piedmont has an average elevation of less than 300 feet (91 m). Gently rolling hills rise to about 1,200 feet (368 m) at its western side.

The largest lakes in Virginia were created by damming the Roanoke River, which flows from the mountains toward Albemarle Sound in North Carolina. Smith Mountain Lake and long, twisting Lake Gaston are fine recreation areas.

Ridges and Valleys

West of the Piedmont is a region called the Ridges and Valleys. It is made up of a series of almost parallel mountain ranges of the huge Appalachian Mountain system. The Appalachians are ancient mountains. Once tall and jagged peaks, they are now rounded and worn. They rarely reach an elevation of more than 5,000 feet (1,524 m).

The first mountains a traveler comes to are the Blue Ridge. In the central part of the state, west of Roanoke, the Blue Ridge range is very narrow, not more than 14 miles (22.5 km) across. Farther south, along the North Carolina border, the mountains are about 70 miles (113 km) across. The highest point in the state lies in this area. It is Mount Rogers, which has an elevation of 5,729 feet (1,746 m). Farther west are the Allegheny Mountains, shared with West Virginia.

Throughout history, the fertile valley between these two mountain ranges has been important. The whole valley is called the Valley of Virginia, but it is broken into several separate valleys by dividing ridges. The northernmost—and largest—valley is the Shenandoah Valley, which is drained by the Shenandoah

Crabtree Falls in the Blue Ridge Mountains

Virginia's Geographical Features

Total area; rank	42,326 sq. mi. (109,625 sq km); 35th
Land; rank	39,598 sq. mi. (102,559 sq km); 37th
Water; rank	2,728 sq. mi. (7,066 sq km); 15th
Inland water; rank	1,000 sq. mi. (2,590 sq km); 22nd
Coastal water; rank	1,728 sq. mi. (4,476 sq km); 5th
Geographic center	5 miles (8 km) southwest of Buckingham
Highest point	Mount Rogers, 5,729 feet (1,746 m)
Lowest point	Sea level along the Atlantic Ocean
Largest city	Virginia Beach
Population; rank	6,216,568 (1990 census); 12th
Record high temperature	110°F (43°C) at Columbia on July 5, 1900, and at Balcony Falls on July 15, 1954
Record low temperature	–30°F (–34°C) at Mountain Lake on January 22, 1985
Average July temperature	75°F (24°C)
Average January temperature	36°F (2°C)
Average annual precipitation	43 inches (109 cm)

River. The name *Shenandoah* is an Indian word meaning "daughter of the stars."

The valley was once an ancient sea. When it receded, it left behind eerie towers of gnarled rock in an area called Natural Chimneys. There are many caverns in the Blue Ridge Mountains with equally twisted formations underground. Luray Caverns, one of the most famous, is also the headquarters of the Shenandoah National Park.

The Blue Ridge Parkway is a popular scenic road that starts in Front Royal as Skyline Drive. When Skyline Drive was opened, it provided a huge panorama of scenes through the mountains. Today, the views are not so panoramic because of pollution in the air, but on days when breezes clear the air, the scenes are still spectacular, especially in autumn color.

The Blue Ridge Parkway goes through the Shenandoah Valley to Great Smoky Mountains National Park in Tennessee. Together, the drive and the parkway make, if not the biggest, certainly the longest, national park. The parkway itself and the beautiful stone bridges passing over it were constructed by workers during the Great Depression of the 1930s.

In a line southwestward from the Shenandoah are five more valleys—Fincastle, Roanoke, New River, Holston, and Clinch. Each valley has a different river draining it and different characteristics. The New River, for example, is actually one of the oldest rivers on the planet. While most rivers disappear as mountains around them are raised and eroded, the New River apparently has existed since the Appalachian Mountains were created.

Cumberland Gap National Park

Cumberland Gap

In the north, the gaps in the Blue Ridge Mountains created by wind and water. They were too high and rough for wagons to traverse. Cumberland Gap in the south is the only reasonably accessible opening through the Appalachian Mountains through most of the East.

Daniel Boone and a group

of workers cut the Wilderness Road through the Cumberland Gap, opening up the western part of what was once part of Virginia. Wagons of pioneers could move from Virginia into the wide-open spaces of Kentucky and the Ohio River Valley.

This historically important area is now Cumberland Gap National Historic Park, which straddles the region where Virginia, Tennessee, and Kentucky join. There's one point in the park, called Tri-State Peak, where a visitor can place two feet and a hand in three different states at once.

Breaks Interstate Park on Pine Mountain is shared by Virginia and Kentucky. The park features the biggest gorge, or canyon, in the eastern part of the nation. The gorge was dug by the Russell Fork River.

Chesapeake Bay

The word *Chesapeake* means "Great Shellfish Bay" in a Native American language. The huge bay was formed when the glaciers of the Ice Age retreated. At that time what eventually became the Susquehanna River of Pennsylvania and Maryland flooded its valley, creating the bay.

Chesapeake Bay is the largest estuary in the United States. It is 193 miles (311 km) long, and its width varies from only 3 miles (4.8 km) to 25 miles (40 km). The Chesapeake Bay Bridge, which is usually clogged on weekends carrying vacationers to the Eastern Shore, spans a section of the bay that is 4.7 miles (7.6 km) wide at Annapolis, Maryland. Because the bay was formed by a river, it has a channel through the center that is deep enough to let ships sail up it.

Seashores and Ponies

A number of slender sandbars known as barrier islands lie along the coast of the Middle Atlantic states. They accumulate sand from the sea and protect the mainland from the harsh waves of the Atlantic. One of these along the Delmarva Peninsula is called Assateague Island. The core of Assateague Island National Seashore, it features 37 miles (60 km) of beautiful beach and huge numbers of shorebirds.

One of the attractions of Assateague is the small wild ponies, which are probably descended from some that swam ashore from a sinking ship hundreds of years ago, or perhaps from some that were hidden there by colonists seeking to avoid taxes. They are usually called Chincoteague ponies, after the adjacent island of Chincoteague. Each year, more ponies are born in the wild than can comfortably live on Assateague. Early in July, they are rounded up and herded across the water to Chincoteague, where they are auctioned off to families who will take good care of them. Author Marguerite Henry wrote a popular children's book about the ponies called *Misty of Chincoteague.* ■

Border Changes on Chesapeake Bay

North of Virginia, a new colony was established under a grant made in 1632 by King Charles I to George Calvert, a Catholic who became the first Lord Baltimore. The king granted Calvert all the land between the 40th parallel of latitude and the low-water mark of the Potomac River. But a fur trader named William Claiborne had already settled Kent Island and several nearby islands that were part of the Maryland colony. He refused to acknowledge that Calvert had any claim to his lands.

Claiborne and his fellow settlers fought what might be called America's first civil war over that land. Several people were killed. It wasn't until 1657 that the Virginia Colony officially recognized the validity of the charter, but they didn't recognize the boundary. Up to the twenty-first century, Virginia and Maryland have continued their squabbles, usually in court, because fishing rights remain important to both states. Occasionally the boundary gets changed by a few feet one way or the other. ◼

Chesapeake Bay is sometimes described as having an 8,000-mile (12,874-km) shoreline. This includes the jagged shores of the bay itself as well as the estuaries of all the rivers that flow into it.

There are more islands in Maryland's part of Chesapeake Bay than there are in Virginia's, but Virginia has one of the most famous—Tangier Island. Settled for centuries, the island's people have led isolated lives and until recently spoke Elizabethan English. Even today, they can be reached only by boat.

Virginia owns the smallest section of the bay and the Eastern Shore. The southern tip of the shore is joined to Norfolk by the Chesapeake Bay Bridge-Tunnel. Started in 1958, this complex of bridges, concrete islands, and tunnels is 17.6 miles (28 km) long. The tunnels dip under the deep channel at the entrance to the bay.

Chesapeake Bay is vulnerable to changes of many kinds. Some years, the populations of jellyfish are so large that all swimming is called off. In 1997, microscopic organisms in the water turned toxic, poisoning fish and forcing the closing of several rivers to fishing. Scientists think the chemical runoff from farms along the bay shores may have caused a chemical change in the organisms.

The biggest problem, however, is that too many people love the bay, its beauty, and its recreational opportunities. The more people build along its shores, the more problems the bay will face.

Climate

In climate, too, Virginia can be regarded as a Middle Atlantic state. It lies at a comfortable middle point between the high heat and humidity of the South and the bitter cold winters of the North.

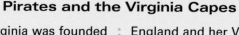

Pirates and the Virginia Capes

Even before Virginia was founded as a colony, word had spread among pirates that its large estuaries and capes offered safety. Some of the buccaneers who sailed Virginia waters were legitimate privateers—owners of private vessels who signed on with the Royal Navy. It was their job to harass and plunder the ships of whatever country England was at war with. The pirates did the same thing, but illegally. Queen Elizabeth I, however, encouraged English pirates, as long as they went after Spanish ships and Spanish towns in the Americas.

When James I came to the throne, he signed a peace treaty with Spain, and pirates began to prey on English ships. As the number of ships that sailed between England and her Virginia colonies increased, their chances of escaping the attentions of pirates decreased. The routes they sailed became known to pirates of all nations as good hunting grounds.

The English often included pirates among the prisoners they shipped to Virginia as punishment. However, this gave pirate captains a wider choice of experienced men for their crews. And those pirate crews didn't always keep to the seas. They sometimes sailed up the rivers and along the Chesapeake, seeking isolated plantations to loot.

The Crown, in an Act of Grace, offered a pardon to pirates for any evil deeds carried out before January 5, 1718. Slowly, piracy disappeared from Virginia and surrounding colonies. ■

The Tidewater, being low and close to the sea, is warmer and more humid than the Piedmont. Both sections are warmer than the mountains.

Virginia's only reliable snow falls in the mountains. Most of Virginia gets little snow, at least not enough to cause long-lasting traffic problems. A good blizzard out of the west or south can snarl traffic for a day or so, then warmer temperatures usually melt the snow. The average annual precipitation is about 43 inches (109 cm), about the same as Texas or New York.

The average temperature in summer stays between 70° and 80° F (21° and 27°C). However, that average is reached by combining cooler temperatures in the mountains and warmer temperatures along the Coastal Plain. Summer temperatures in the Piedmont range between 85°F (30°C) and 95°F (35°C). The hottest temperature on record is 110°F (43°C) at Columbia on July 5, 1900, and at Balcony Falls on July 15, 1954.

The average temperature in January is about 36°F (2°C). The coldest on record was −30°F (−34°C) at Mountain Lake on January 22, 1985.

Mountain peaks in Otter

"Fair Meadows and Goodly Tall Trees"

Scholar George Percy was aboard one of the ships that arrived in Virginia in 1607. He called what he saw a land of "fair meadows and goodly tall trees." He saw forests of densely growing pines, oak, ash, and walnut.

The colonists gave the name "Virginia" to several of the plants they discovered. Virginia creeper is an ivylike plant that grows on buildings and fences, and even on trees. The Virginia bluebell is cultivated in gardens and grows wild in moist woods. It has pink bell-shaped blossoms that turn blue as they age.

The colonists found small grasslands too. Growing in those grasslands were plants that came to be called tobacco. The Indians

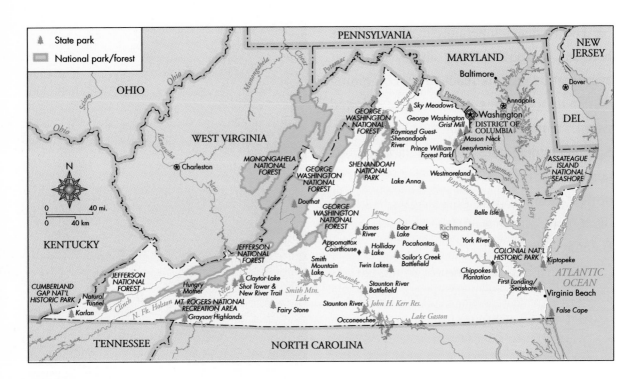

Virginia's parks and forests

also grew maize, or corn. The grasslands were home to the red deer and fallow deer, which colonists hunted for food. Farther west, in the mountains, the colonists hunted small black bears.

Today, there are two national forests in western Virginia—George Washington and Jefferson. Prince William Forest is owned by the federal government but is not designated as a national park or national forest.

The forests of Virginia are home to many birds, most notably the wild turkey. There are probably more turkeys in Virginia than in Massachusetts, where Thanksgiving started.

Shenandoah has twelve different species of salamander—an unusual situation for these elusive creatures. Virginia has three subspecies of poisonous snake—the timber rattler, the northern copperhead, and the eastern cottonmouth.

Chesapeake Bay is surrounded by swamps and bogs that the colonists found teeming with waterbirds. The bay itself swarmed with fish and shellfish, especially oysters and crabs. The wildlife today does not teem quite so much. Too many people have moved to the shore.

False Cape State Park in southeastern Virginia can't be reached by car. Visitors must hike to it through Back Bay National Wildlife Refuge, but it's worth the trip to get a close look at the many bird and small mammal species.

CHAPTER SIX

From Mountain to Sea

City Hall in Alexandria

Virginia is a state of cities and seas, mountains and rolling hills. Its cities have grown in response to industry and reaction. Most of them are in the Tidewater, where the colonists built first. Beyond the Fall Line, only Roanoke has any real size.

No matter where a visitor goes in Virginia, however, hospitality can be enjoyed. In northern Virginia, around Washington, D.C., newcomers are less caught up in the old traditions of the state than many longtime residents are. But that doesn't mean that the northern Virginians lack hospitality.

On the Potomac's Edge

Alexandria is a colonial city in Northern Virginia. It lies across the Potomac River, south of Washington, D.C. Founded by the General Assembly on land owned by a man named John Alexander, it gained early recognition as a port and a slave-trading center. George Washington, who helped survey the site, lived nearby at

Opposite: Spring forests on Appalachian ridges

Mount Vernon, and as the new town grew, he spent considerable time there. Visitors today can see where he frequently walked, went to church, and joined other men at a club.

After the American Revolution, when the new country was establishing a national capital, Congress drew a square across the Potomac River and called it the District of Columbia. Virginia agreed that the nation could have Alexandria and nearby Arlington. However, the growing government paid little attention to the land on the other side of the river, and Virginia wanted its riverfront back. In 1846, ninety-seven years after its founding, Alexandria became part of Virginia again.

Perhaps because of the government's neglect, the oldest part of Alexandria still stands. Old Town is filled with fascinating colonial row houses (one of them only a few feet wide), brick streets, and lovely old city buildings. Along the riverfront, a huge old World War I torpedo factory has been turned into shops, galleries, and restaurants. The city's government has kept the look of the old city in its new public buildings in Old Town.

Neighboring Arlington was farm country while Alexandria was developing and for many years afterward. Today, however, it is a major center of

Alexandria's Old Town

Arlington National Cemetery

Overlooking the Potomac River and Washington, D.C., is a beautiful columned mansion called Arlington House. It was built in 1802 by George Washington Parke Custis to honor the man who raised him— George Washington. He filled the house with memorabilia of the first president and invited people to visit.

Custis's daughter, Mary, married Robert E. Lee, a soldier in the United States Army. When Lee was forced by the secession of his beloved Virginia to choose sides in the Civil War, he became leader of the Confederate forces. Within days, the Union Army confiscated his plantation. During the war, Mary missed paying taxes because she was ill, and the Union claimed the mansion and its lands. The Union began to bury its soldiers on the slopes of the hill below the mansion, which gradually turned into Arlington National Cemetery. In later years, the bodies of Confederate soldiers were also brought to the cemetery.

Today, Arlington is the largest national cemetery and one of the most-visited national sites. It is the burial place of President John F. Kennedy. It includes the Tomb of the Unknowns, which holds the remains of unidentified men who died in the United States's wars. This marble tomb is guarded by representatives of the four branches of the U.S. military. Christa McAuliffe, the teacher who was killed aboard the explosion of the space shuttle *Challenger* in 1986, is also buried in Arlington. Other special memorials were joined in 1997 by the spectacular new Women in Military Service for America Memorial. ■

international business, conveniently located just across Memorial Bridge from the capital.

Between Alexandria and Arlington stands one of the military centers of the world—the Pentagon. Housing the U.S. Department of Defense, it was built during World War II. This five-sided building is one of the largest office buildings in the world. Almost 30,000 people work there. Some of them use golf carts to get from one section to another. Many Pentagon workers live in a huge complex called Crystal City, which features many apartment and office buildings built primarily of glass.

Arlington House, also called the Custis Mansion, stands on a hill above Arlington National Cemetery and is visible from Washington, D.C. Arlington developed around this estate. When it was taken over by the federal government in 1864, Fort Whipple was built on land behind the mansion. It was later renamed Fort Myer and became the headquarters of a cavalry unit. It was the last army fort to house horses for cavalry officers (the cavalry now rides in tanks), and the first military base to have military aircraft. It was at Fort Myer that Orville and Wilbur Wright demonstrated the military version of their new-fangled airplane in 1909.

A car coming into Virginia across Memorial Bridge circles the Iwo Jima Memorial. Officially the U.S. Marine Memorial, the statue shows six soldiers raising the flag on the island of Iwo Jima during World War II. The odd thing about the breathtaking statue is that only five of the six figures are visible at any one time to someone walking around it.

Perhaps you've heard the phrase "inside the Beltway." That refers to all the government and political activities that take place

The Iwo Jima
Memorial

around Washington, D.C., and inside Highway 495, or the Beltway. It circles through Virginia and Maryland.

As northern Virginia suburbs—both inside and outside the Beltway—have grown, many old communities have ballooned. An intriguing mixture of old and new, they always have the problem of keeping the old while allowing for the increase in traffic, and the need for new schools and housing. Such growth has created Tyson's Corner, now one of the biggest shopping complexes anywhere in the East.

Farther northwest in Fairfax County is one urban planner's solution—the incredible new city of Reston. An area that con-

Dulles International Airport

Will It Work?

An experiment is in progress in the vicinity of Dulles International Airport. A privately owned highway called the Dulles Greenway may be used—for a fee, called a toll—by drivers who do not want to deal with the congestion on the main public roads from Washington, D.C., to Dulles. Some people think that such private roads may be an answer to keeping taxes low, as taxes won't have to be used to build other roads. Others think that such additional roads are bad for the environment. ■

sisted of open fields in 1962 now has close to 50,000 residents living, working, and shopping in beautiful small communities separated by open forestland.

The major airports in northern Virginia are Washington National, located near the Pentagon, and Dulles International, bordering western Fairfax County. In 1998, Washington National Airport was officially renamed Ronald Reagan Washington National Airport, after former President Reagan, on his 87th birthday.

Away from the U.S. Capital

Not very far out of Arlington and Fairfax County are old towns that until recent decades were as isolated from capital life as towns in the distant mountains. Now, however, they are within the reach of commuters and changes are rapid.

George Washington's Canals

As the new United States grew north of the Ohio River, Virginians—led by George Washington himself—knew that the young United States would hold together only if the new areas could reach the markets of the older East. They needed some way to reach the Ohio River. Washington's dream took the form of the James River and Kanawha Canal, which could carry shipments past the blockading Fall Line.

The first segment, built from Richmond to Westham in 1790, was the nation's first commercial canal. It was periodically lengthened until, just before the Civil War, it reached beyond Lynchburg in the foothills of the Blue Ridge Mountains. However, the James River and Kanawha Canal never quite reached the Kanawha River in what is now West Virginia. Major parts of the canal were destroyed by General Philip Sheridan's troops in 1865, and it was never reopened. In Richmond, the remains of the canal are being cleaned up and developed as a luxurious riverfront retail area. ■

The Old Town section of Manassas, for example, is being restored with a focus on the old Railroad Express Station. In the early 1990s, the Walt Disney Corporation planned a recreational and historical park, to be called Disney's America, for an area west of Manassas where major battles of the Civil War occurred. Many people objected on the grounds that important historical sites could become overrun with tourists. In 1994, Disney dropped the idea.

Fredericksburg, by the falls of the Rappahannock River, is a colonial city where George Washington spent much time. He lived on a nearby farm. His brother owned the Rising Sun Tavern, which is still open for business. In her later years, his mother, Mary Ball Washington, lived in a charming house that is now open to the public.

Richmond was a major port in the first part of the nineteenth century. It dealt especially with coffee from South America. Along with the coffee, many ships carried round rocks as ballast, or extra weight, to keep the ship balanced. Richmond's streets were paved with these cobblestones from another continent. These ships from South America and other places carried away the vast tobacco crops that grew in the South.

A number of places in Richmond, as might be expected, were involved in the Civil War. The house where Jefferson Davis lived is called the White House of the Confederacy. Statues of the heroes of the Confederacy stand along Monument Avenue. Richmond National Battlefield Park is located where Chimborazo, perhaps the largest military hospital ever built, used to stand. The Museum of the Confederacy has a renowned collection of Civil War art and records.

The Virginia State Fair is held in Richmond each year in late September or early October.

The Watery Roads

Five major cities thrive on the huge body of water called Hampton Roads—Norfolk, Newport News, Portsmouth, Chesapeake, and Hampton. Waterfront is everywhere, making the area a joy to anyone who likes the smell of the sea.

Newport News was named for Captain Newport, who was regarded as the admiral of the Virginia Colony. The odd name "News" is probably a version of the last name of Sir William Newce, one of the Irishmen who helped settle the area in 1621.

Hampton, which has existed (in various forms, because it was

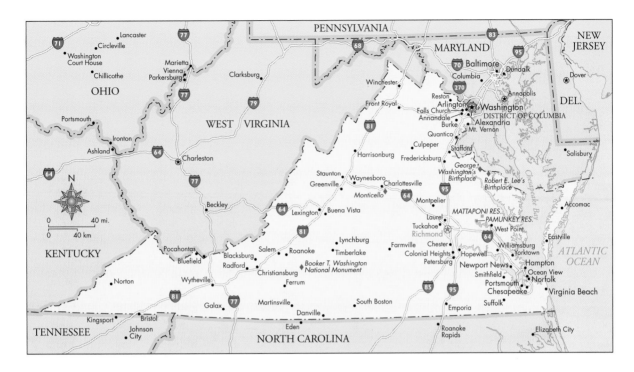

Virginia's cities and interstates

burned down twice) since 1609, is synonymous with the military and education. It was the location of the first free school in America. Later, Hampton Normal and Agricultural Institute was created for African-Americans and has turned into Hampton University. Nearby, NASA's Langley Research Center boasts the Virginia Air and Space Center.

The city of Norfolk began in 1682, mainly as a collection of warehouses for storing, shipping, and receiving tobacco. The town became an important port city, serving both Virginia and the Carolinas. Norfolk carpenters were kept busy repairing ships that came into port, and by the 1730s began to build ships, too, using huge old trees from Great Dismal Swamp nearby. In 1907, Norfolk won the right to hold a large exposition commemorating the 300th anniversary of the founding of Jamestown.

Much of the Norfolk area consists of the Norfolk Naval Base

Virginia Beach

and the adjoining Norfolk Naval Air Station. Together, they make up the largest naval base in the world. It is home to the United States Atlantic Fleet, meaning that hundreds of submarines, destroyers, aircraft carriers, and many smaller ships are often seen in the harbor.

Where there is water, there will usually be resorts, and Hampton Roads is no different. Ocean View on the Roads was one of the first resorts in the state. It was later followed by Virginia Beach, located east of Norfolk, on the coast. With 38 miles (61 km) of oceanfront, it's no wonder that the city developed into a resort. Since merging with an entire county in 1963, the city's boundaries reach to the border of North Carolina. Virginia Beach has grown so much that it is now the largest city in the state.

The Stars of Colonial History

The heart of Virginia history lies on the peninsula between the York and the James Rivers. The colony was founded at Jamestown, or James Citie on the James, and it became a state with the defeat of the British at Yorktown about 20 miles (32 km) away on the other side of the peninsula. The federal government has joined the two in Colonial National Historical Park, which also lies adjacent to Williamsburg, the second capital.

Little remains of the original Jamestown on the island, though foundations of some of the old buildings have been excavated. A discovery in 1996 yielded numerous artifacts of the early days which are now preserved in a museum. Nearby is Jamestown

The Remaking of Williamsburg

After the capital was moved to Richmond in 1780, Williamsburg began to deteriorate, except around the College of William and Mary. The city of Williamsburg continued to develop while the colonial portion fell apart. In 1926, the minister at Bruton Parish Church persuaded oil billionaire John D. Rockefeller to become involved in the restoration of the capital that played such an important part in American history.

About 3,000 acres (1,200 ha) of colonial Williamsburg have been cleaned up, restored, or, when necessary, reconstructed. The Capitol and the Governor's Palace are decorated and furnished as they would have been at the time they were in use in the 1700s. Colonial Williamsburg is a living museum with people dressing in costume and carrying out the normal activities of life in a colonial city. Research is still continuing, and changes are made as new facts about the old city are discovered. ■

Festival Park, a re-creation of James Citie. In 1957, on the 350th anniversary of the founding of Jamestown, British queen Elizabeth II visited Jamestown.

Across the peninsula, a tall, narrow monument stands at Yorktown, marking the victory of George Washington's Continental Army over British forces on October 19, 1781. The marble shaft was built in 1907, on the 300th anniversary of the founding of Virginia. It is surrounded by Yorktown Victory Center, which includes replicas of the early buildings and demonstrations of how the colonists lived.

Plantation Life Relived

The oldest plantation in the United States is Shirley (originally Shirley Hundred). Founded in 1613, the James River grant made to

Shirley Plantation

Monticello

Probably the most famous of the plantations was the creation of one dedicated man—Thomas Jefferson. He was dedicated both to the new nation he helped create and to fostering beauty in that new nation.

Jefferson, born at Albemarle, designed his red-brick and white-columned home, Monticello (which means "Little Mountain" in Italian), near Charlottesville, starting in 1768. He continued working on the estate until his death.

Jefferson spent five years in France following the Revolutionary War and returned with new ideas. He revamped the house greatly, ending up with a house in which each of the 35 rooms is a different shape. He is known as one of the great architects of early Virginia. ■

Sir Thomas West and his brothers was the first the king made to an individual. The beautiful red-brick house that can still be seen today was built in 1723. During the Civil War, Shirley served as a Union military hospital.

Richard Henry Lee and his brother Francis, both of whom signed the Declaration of Independence, were born at Stratford Hall, on the Potomac River, as was General Robert E. Lee. Today, Stratford is owned by the Robert E. Lee Memorial Foundation.

Carter's Grove has long been shown as an example of a "lifestyle of the rich and famous" in Virginia. Recently, archaeologists discovered the remnants of the plantation's extensive slave quarters. They have been reconstructed and are now an important record of slave life during the colonial period.

Several presidents came from plantations that still exist. William Henry Harrison was born at Berkeley Plantation, which was built by his father, a signer of the Declaration of Independence. Harrison also owned Sherwood Forest, where John Tyler lived.

In 1819, Thomas Jefferson founded the University of Virginia at Charlottesville. The original buildings of this fine university, which he also designed, look very much like his Monticello. The beautiful campus (called the "grounds") is a World Heritage Site, deemed by the United Nations as a place worth preserving for humanity.

Jefferson also designed Bremo, a plantation home for General John Hartwell Cocke, who had helped Jefferson found the university. Cocke was famed (and sometimes reviled) for preparing the slaves on his plantation for freedom. Bremo has one of the few chapels on plantations where slaves could worship.

West of Charlottesville is the small town of Greenville, where popular radio singer Kate Smith was born. Her booming rendition of "God Bless America" made both the song and Kate Smith famous.

Southwest of Charlottesville is Lynchburg, in the foothills of the Blue Ridge Mountains. It was connected to Richmond by the James River and Kanawha Canal in 1840. For two decades, the canal was the main road for both business and pleasure from the mountains to the sea, a distance of 156 miles (251 km). A number of colleges are located at Lynchburg, including Liberty College, which was founded in 1971 by conservative minister Jerry Falwell. Randolph-Macon Woman's College, founded in 1891, was Virginia's first college for women.

Northwest of Lynchburg is Lexington, another famed university city. Lexington is home to both the Virginia Military Institute and Washington and Lee University.

In 1796, George Washington made a major financial contribution to what was then the all-male Augusta Academy. The school gratefully changed its name to Washington Academy. When Robert E. Lee became president of the school after the Civil War, it again changed its name. The great general and his wife are buried in a crypt beneath the school's chapel. Lee's horse Traveler is buried in the grounds. Today, Washington and Lee welcomes both men and women.

Virginia Military Institute (VMI) was founded in 1839 and has been the primary school for southern military officers ever since. It was the first state-supported military college in the United States. The cadet corps fought (and mostly died) in the Civil War's Battle of New Market in 1864.

Two important Virginia names are associated with VMI. George C. Marshall was the U.S. secretary of state after World War II. It was his idea, called the Marshall Plan, that helped the economies of European and Asian countries devastated by the war, to get moving again. He was awarded the 1953 Nobel Peace Prize for his work. Though he was born in Pennsylvania, Marshall's family were Virginians and he graduated from VMI. The George C. Marshall Museum is located in Lexington.

Cadets at Virginia Military Institute

Nearby is the museum/home of VMI graduate and professor General Thomas "Stonewall" Jackson, of Civil War fame. He earned his nickname during the First Battle of Manassas by keeping his brigade firmly blocking the advance of Union troops.

Into the Blue Ridge

Roanoke is the gateway to the southwestern triangle that reaches out toward the Cumberland Gap. In 1880, Roanoke was a village called Big Lick. Then the Norfolk and Western Railroad decided to put their machine shops there. Starting in 1882, the railroad carried mountain coal to Norfolk, from which it went all over the United States.

Today, the "Capital of the Blue Ridge" has about 100,000 residents. It has become an art and history center of the beautiful mountain region. Much of the city climbs the side of Mill Mountain, which stands apart from the Blue Ridge and Allegheny mountain ranges surrounding the city. Roanoke has a collection of museums that showcase the arts, crafts, and history of the Ridges and Valleys region.

Up from Slavery

South of Roanoke is the Booker T. Washington National Monument. This African-American hero was born into slavery in a one-room cabin on a tobacco farm in Franklin County. Son of the farm's cook, he wanted desperately to learn, but teaching slaves was illegal. After the slaves were freed, young Washington heard about a school for black people in Hampton. He made his way there on foot and became a student at the Hampton Institute (now Hampton University). Becoming a teacher there, he was asked to head the new Tuskegee Institute in Alabama. He turned that school for African-Americans from an idea into a highly regarded college, now Tuskegee University.

Washington's autobiography, *Up from Slavery,* became immensely popular and encouraged many black people to seek further education. The shack where Washington was born disappeared long ago, but the National Monument dedicated to him has a reconstruction of his earliest home. ■

Although thousands of people have gone westward through Cumberland Gap, that region of Virginia is still somewhat isolated today because there are no major roads into it.

Near the North Carolina border, forming a triangle with Roanoke and Lynchburg, is a small city called Danville, which was briefly the capital of the Confederacy. After Richmond burned, for the seven days from April 3 to 10, 1865, the doomed nation's government was moved to Danville, where the leaders met in a mansion that became the Danville Public Library.

Perhaps the most famous native of Danville was Nancy Langhorne, who became Lady Astor in England. When her husband, a member of Parliament, was elevated to the House of Lords in 1919, she ran for his seat and became the first woman to serve in the British Parliament. Danville has a Lady Astor Street.

The Appalachian National Scenic Trail

In 1921, individuals and states began to develop a wondrous hiking trail that traverses the crests and valleys of the Appalachian Mountain system from Maine to Georgia. In 1968, Congress gave official approval to a 2,000-mile (3,200-km) trail, calling it the Appalachian National Scenic Trail. A truly devoted hiker may make the full journey in five or six months, camping out at night. But most hikers find shorter trips easier to handle.

One of Virginia's attractive portions of the national trail is Mount Rogers National Recreation Area, which centers around Mount Rogers, Virginia's highest peak. Another is Shenandoah National Park.

CHAPTER SEVEN

Governing
Old Dominion

Virginia calls itself a commonwealth, rather than a state. A commonwealth is by definition a body of people who agree to live under law and work for the common good of the governed.

The state has ninety-five counties, plus forty independent cities that do not belong to specific counties—an unusual arrangement. Arlington, across the Potomac from Washington, D.C., is an entire county, and at only 24 square miles (62 sq km), it is the state's smallest county. It is a county without a city. Right next to it is Alexandria, which is a city without a county.

The largest county by population is Fairfax in northern Virginia. It has almost a million people. The smallest by population is Highland, the little mountainous area that projects northward into West Virginia. It has little more than 2,500 people. In area, the largest county is Augusta, with 972 square miles (2,517 sq km). Second in area is Pittsylvania County.

Monument Avenue in Richmond

Opposite: The George Washington statue in front of the Old Richmond City Hall

Virginia's State Symbols

State bird: Cardinal This red songbird (left) was taken to England as a caged bird in the early years, where it was known as the Virginia nightingale. It was chosen as the state bird in 1950.

State dog: American foxhound Chosen as the state dog in 1966, it is one of only four breeds that have developed in America. All the foxhounds were bred from dogs that George Washington brought into the colony.

State flower and tree: Flowering dogwood The state flower (right) was chosen in 1918, though the tree that it grows on was not chosen as the state tree until 1956. The South's dogwood is not like the North's. It is a tall tree with large waxy evergreen leaves. Around each tiny cluster of flowers are what look like large white petals, but they are actually specialized leaves.

The State Flag and Seal

In 1861, Virginia established a state flag design that virtually matches the design used today. Today's flag is deep blue with a circular white center, and has the Great Seal of the Commonwealth on both sides. A salute to the Virginia flag, adopted in 1954, says, "I salute the flag of Virginia, with reverence and patriotic devotion to the 'Mother of States and Statesmen,' which it represents—the 'Old Dominion,' where liberty and independence were born."

The front side of the state seal has the Roman goddess Virtue with her foot on the chest of Tyranny with the motto: *Sic Semper Tyrannis* (Thus Always to Tyrants). The back of the seal shows Roman goddesses—Liberty, Eternity, and Fruitfulness—with the Latin word *Perservando* (by perservering) above. ▪

State shell: Oyster Adopted in 1974, this shelled creature represents Virginia's position on Chesapeake Bay.

State beverage: Milk Because of its many uses, Virginia's General Assembly adopted milk as the state beverage in 1982.

State boat: Chesapeake Bay deadrise Adopted in 1988, it is described as "a wooden boat with a sharp bow, a tiny cabin, and a long cockpit. It can operate nearly everywhere on the bay for crabbing, oystering, and fishing."

State insect: Tiger swallowtail butterfly This common butterfly (right) with black and yellow stripes was adopted in 1991.

State fish: Brook trout In 1993, the General Assembly recognized this fighting fish of Virginia's mountain rivers and streams.

State fossil: _Chesapecten jeffersonius_ Chosen in 1993, this ancient shelled animal was originally found in North America. The fossil was named in honor of Virginian Thomas Jefferson, who was fascinated with natural history.

State folk dance: Square dance A descendant of English and French dances, the square dance has strong roots in American folk and Virginia culture. It was adopted in 1991. ■

Virginia's State Song

At present, there is no Virginia state song. In 1997, the General Assembly voted to cancel the 1940 adoption of "Carry Me Back to Old Virginia," which was written by James A. Bland in 1875. The move, which was initiated in 1970, was in response to criticism that the words of the song "glorified" slavery. The song contained a number of objectionable phrases. ■

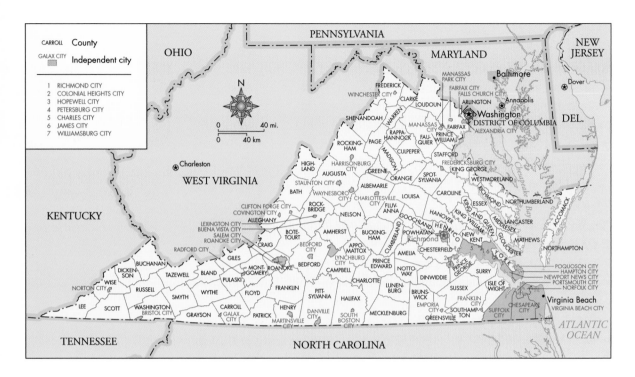

Virginia's counties

The Saga of the Capitols

Virginia's legislature, founded in 1619, was the first democratically elected body in the Western Hemisphere. It was called the House of Burgesses until 1775. *Burgess* is an old English word meaning a citizen of a borough, or a region of the countryside. So a burgess was a person who represented his borough or district. At the beginning there were eleven districts (basically the plantations), each with two representatives.

The first statehouse was the home of Governor Sir John Harvey. Its remains are still visible at Jamestown. From 1656 to 1665, the legislators met in a second statehouse, which probably burned, and a tavern. Another statehouse in Jamestown was destroyed during Bacon's Rebellion, in 1676. The entire settlement—which con-

The College of William and Mary

The Virginia Reel

The Virginia reel is an American country dance that evolved from a group dance brought from England as the "Sir Roger de Coverley." Couples stand in a line, and the couple at one end dance with each other and then with the other people down each side of the line, stopping at the end. Gradually, each couple becomes the head couple. The Virginia reel is just one of the many square dances that many people enjoy. In 1991, Virginia's General Assembly named the square dance the state dance. ■

sisted of probably no more than eighteen houses—burned at that time, but was quickly rebuilt. A fourth statehouse survived until 1699, when it too burned, though not during a rebellion.

The colonial government chose to move the capital to Middle Plantation, where the College of William and Mary had been started. The oldest building at William and Mary was designed by Christopher Wren, the architect who rebuilt much of London after the Great Fire of 1666. The governing body changed Middle Plantation's name to Williamsburg.

Unlike Jamestown, which grew without a plan (and faded away in the same way), Williamsburg was designed for growth. The plan for the town was made by Governor Francis Nicholson. He called for red-brick buildings laid out in a style that made the

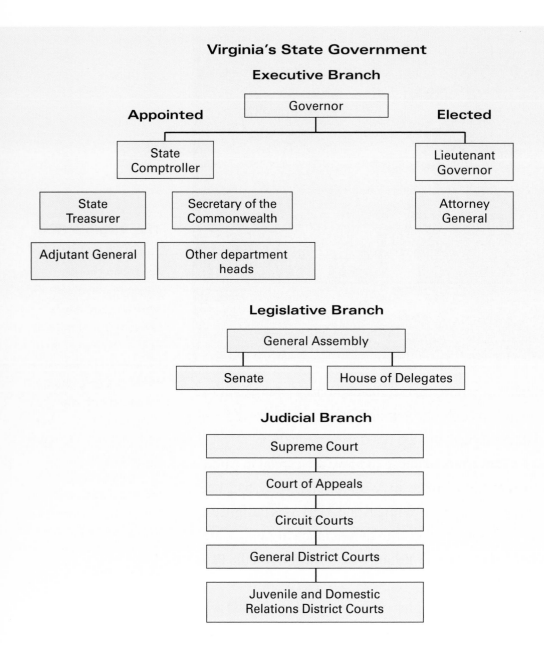

Virginia's State Government

Executive Branch

	Governor	
Appointed		**Elected**

State Comptroller

Lieutenant Governor

State Treasurer

Secretary of the Commonwealth

Attorney General

Adjutant General

Other department heads

Legislative Branch

General Assembly

Senate

House of Delegates

Judicial Branch

Supreme Court

Court of Appeals

Circuit Courts

General District Courts

Juvenile and Domestic Relations District Courts

Women in the House of Delegates

The first women to serve in the House of Delegates were Helen Timmons Henderson and Sarah Lee Fain (right). They were elected to the House of Delegates in 1924, five years after the Nineteenth Amendment giving women the right to vote was proposed by Congress. Virginia politicians did not ratify, or approve, this amendment until 1952, but it had become law in 1920, after being ratified by enough other states. Sarah Lee Fain went on to be re-elected, the first woman in the legislature of a southern state to be so honored. ■

town look as if it belonged to the Italian Renaissance. His own house was called the Palace.

The legislature met in the buildings of the College of William and Mary for the five years that it took to build the new capitol. It had better luck than all the earlier ones, not burning down until 1747. The capitol built next was in use in 1776 when the people of Virginia declared themselves free of Great Britain.

Modern State Government

When Virginia became part of the new United States of America, its old House of Burgesses was replaced by the House of Delegates. The old Council of State became the Senate. Together, the Senate and the House of Delegates make up the General Assembly. There are 40 senators, who serve four-year terms, and 100 delegates, elected for two-year terms.

Until 1851, the governor was chosen by the General Assembly. Since then that position has been filled by popular vote. The top three offices are elective—governor, lieutenant governor, and attor-

Virginia's Governors

Name	Party	Term	Name	Party	Term
Patrick Henry	None	1776–1779	Wilson Cary Nicholas	Dem.-Rep.	1814–1816
Thomas Jefferson	None	1779–1781	James Patton Preston	Dem.-Rep.	1816–1819
William Fleming	None	1781	Thomas Mann Randolph	Dem.-Rep.	1819–1822
Thomas Nelson Jr.	None	1781	James Pleasants	Dem.-Rep.	1822–1825
Benjamin Harrison	None	1781–1784	John Tyler Jr.	Dem.-Rep.	1825–1827
Patrick Henry	None	1784–1786	William Branch Giles	Dem.	1827–1830
Edmund Randolph	None	1786–1788	John Floyd	Dem.	1830–1834
Beverley Randolph	None	1788–1791	Littleton Waller Tazewell	Whig	1834–1836
Henry Lee	Federalist	1791–1794	Wyndham Robertson	Whig	1836–1837
Robert Brooke	Dem.-Rep.	1794–1796	David Campbell	Dem.	1837–1840
James Wood	Dem.-Rep.	1796–1799	Thomas Walker Gilmer	Whig	1840–1841
James Monroe	Dem.-Rep.	1799–1802	John Mercer Patton	Whig	1841
John Page	Dem.-Rep.	1802–1805	John Rutherford	Whig	1841–1842
William H. Cabell	Dem.-Rep.	1805–1808	John Munford Gregory	Whig	1842–1843
John Tyler Sr.	Dem.-Rep.	1808–1811	James McDowell	Dem.	1843–1846
James Monroe	Dem.-Rep.	1811	William Smith	Dem.	1846–1849
George William Smith	Dem.-Rep.	1811	John Buchanan Floyd	Dem.	1849–1852
Peyton Randolph	Dem.-Rep.	1811–1812	Joseph Johnson	Dem.	1852–1856
James Barbour	Dem.-Rep.	1812–1814	Henry A. Wise	Dem.	1856–1860

ney general. The governor may serve only one four-year term, but holders of the other elective offices can be re-elected. In the election of 1997, all three offices went to Republicans for the first time in the state's history.

The seven justices on the state's Supreme Court are elected to serve twelve-year terms. Since 1985 there has been a ten-member Court of Appeals, with members elected for eight years. They review decisions made by the lower courts, which include 122 courts in 31 regions called circuits. Circuit court judges are named by the General Assembly.

Unlike many states, Virginia has rewritten its constitution sev-

Name	Party	Term	Name	Party	Term
John Letcher	Dem.	1860–1864	John Garland Pollard	Dem.	1930–1934
William Smith	Dem.	1864–1865	George C. Peery	Dem.	1934–1938
Francis H. Pierpont	Rep.	1865–1868	James H. Price	Dem.	1938–1942
Henry H. Wells	Rep.	1868–1869	Colgate W. Darden Jr.	Dem.	1942–1946
Gilbert C. Walker	Rep.	1869–1874	William M. Tuck	Dem.	1946–1950
James L. Kemper	Dem.	1874–1878	John S. Battle	Dem.	1950–1954
Frederick W. M. Holliday	Dem.	1878–1882	Thomas B. Stanley	Dem.	1954–1958
William E. Cameron	R.-Rep.	1882–1886	J. Lindsay Almond Jr.	Dem.	1958–1962
Fitzhugh Lee	Dem.	1886–1890	Albertis S. Harrison Jr.	Dem.	1962–1966
Philip W. McKinney	Dem.	1890–1894	Mills E. Godwin Jr.	Dem.	1966–1970
Charles T. O'Ferrall	Dem.	1894–1898	A. Linwood Holton Jr.	Rep.	1970–1974
James Hoge Tyler	Dem.	1898–1902	Mills E. Godwin Jr.	Rep.	1974–1978
Andrew Jackson Montague	Dem.	1902–1906	John N. Dalton	Rep.	1978–1982
Claude A. Swanson	Dem.	1906–1910	Charles S. Robb	Dem.	1982–1986
William Hodges Mann	Dem.	1910–1914	Gerald L. Baliles	Dem.	1986–1990
Henry Carter Stuart	Dem.	1914–1918	L. Douglas Wilder	Dem.	1990–1994
Westmoreland Davis	Dem.	1918–1922	George Allen	Rep.	1994–1998
Elbert Lee Trinkle	Dem.	1922–1926	James S. Gilmore III	Rep.	1998–
Harry Flood Byrd	Dem.	1926–1930			

eral times. Its newest constitution was approved in 1971. On the national level, Virginia sends two senators and eleven representatives to Congress.

The New Capital at Richmond

During the American Revolution, Virginians made Richmond, the city built at the Fall Line of the James River, their new capital city. Thomas Jefferson designed the capitol after an ancient Roman temple in France. This building is still the core of a group of structures that now make up the capitol, with the Senate chamber and the House of Delegates in newer wings built out at each side.

Richmond's Jackson Ward

There isn't much of really old Richmond left because most of it was destroyed by fires set when Union forces took over the city. Some of Richmond, however, has historic significance, such as the area called the Jackson Ward. Though no longer a political area, or ward, it was called that in the days of segregation of the races. Jackson Ward was home to many African-Americans, both poor and well-off, who did the best they could for their part of the state's capital. The area is now designated as a historic district.

It has theaters built in the days when black people could not attend public gatherings with white people. Sections of the district contain rows of small, neat houses designed by black architects to house middle-class families. Also in the historic district is the birthplace of dancer Bill Robinson, better known as "Bojangles." Banker Maggie Lena Walker's home is a National Historic Site within the district, and it was largely due to her influence that Jackson Ward developed pride in itself. ■

Richmond National Battlefield Park

National Parks, National History

The federal government owns about 9.4 percent of Virginia's land. Some of that land is used for government buildings, such as the Central Intelligence Agency (CIA). But it also includes wonderful scenery and fascinating history.

Federal sites vary from the solemn grandeur of Arlington National Cemetery to the Mount Rogers Recreation Area in the southwest. They include such historic sites as Appomattox Court House, Petersburg National Battlefield, and Manassas and Richmond National Battlefield Parks.

Mount Vernon

An obvious place is missing from the list of federal lands in Virginia—Mount Vernon, the home of President George Washington, on the Potomac River. After both George and Martha Washington died, the estate was in the hands of descendants of his brother.

Little care was taken of it until the 1850s, when an organization of women under Ann Pamela Cunningham of South Carolina decided that the home of the "Father of Our Country" needed to be preserved. The women raised funds to buy the home. Work on its restoration was stopped during the Civil War, but the main house, the nearby grounds, and the kitchen building at Mount Vernon now look much as they did during Washington's lifetime. ▪

At Quantico, policemen from all over the nation come to train at the Federal Bureau of Investigation's special training school. Also at Quantico is the Quantico Marine Corps Reservation, where U.S. Marine recruits are put through tough training.

CHAPTER EIGHT

Tobacco, Technology, and Tourism

n its earliest years, Virginia's entire economy was based on plantations. We think now of plantations as fancy estates with beautiful houses, all maintained by slaves. But basically a plantation was just a large farm, often with a single crop as the main economic product.

Each plantation was independent, with all its craftspeople and laborers living on the plantation. The owners of these plantations lived in luxury, though many of them worked hard to organize the operation for everyone. The early plantations all lay along one of the major rivers. Tobacco grown on the land was shipped to England, and luxury goods and other items that the colony could not produce were shipped back.

At first, manufacturing was forbidden in the colony so that the colonists would be forced to import all manufactured goods from England. They were also forced to sell their tobacco and other products at prices set in England—a fact they began to resent.

Tobacco growing at Colonial Williamsburg

Tobacco Growing

Christopher Columbus took tobacco back to Europe from the Americas, and Spanish sailors quickly introduced the habit of smoking it. Many people smoked tobacco for its supposed medicinal benefits—though they didn't know what those benefits might

Opposite: Harvesting oysters from the James River

Tobacco ships in the James River

be. Others just found pleasure in it. King James I began to tax it heavily.

It was John Rolfe who planted a milder species of tobacco plant in Virginia than the Indians had used. He had obtained the seeds from the Caribbean. When he sent his first crop to England in 1615, the Virginia Colony made its first profit. Virginia tobacco has ever since been the preferred tobacco the world over.

Rolfe's seeds were quickly planted in every patch of ground available to eager Virginians: The London Company offered land to any Englishman who would go to Virginia and plant tobacco. In the six years after 1619, more than four thousand Englishmen moved to the colony. They could own land there whereas they could not own land back home.

Tobacco was the mainstay of the state when other things fell apart. After the Civil War, it was tobacco that kept Virginia's economy alive while everything else was failing.

A man from Lynchburg, James A. Bonsack, invented the cigarette-making machine in 1880. This invention turned tobacco into an even bigger business.

R. J. (Richard Joshua) Reynolds, founder of the R. J. Reynolds Tobacco Company, was born in Patrick County. After the Civil War, he became a major trader in tobacco, but soon took his business to North Carolina, where he started R. J. Reynolds Tobacco. Until 1999, it was part of the giant corporation called RJR Nabisco.

The world's largest independent seller of tobacco leaves is still located in Richmond. Universal Corporation buys from tobacco growers and sells to the big tobacco companies. Although Americans are cutting back on smoking, the rest of the world still buys great quantities of Virginia tobacco.

A farm near Harrisonburg

Other Agriculture

In the 1840s, newcomers to Virginia began to show local farmers that they didn't have to depend on tobacco. Gradually, Tidewater Virginia became a major source of fresh fruits and vegetables for the nation. This type of farming, called truck farming, continued after the Civil War because it did not require the slave labor needed to grow tobacco.

In today's agriculture, Vir-

The Reaper

Rockbridge County's Cyrus Hall McCormick invented the reaper, which cut grain in fields, in 1831. Fifteen years later, he decided that to continue making improvements and to sell his machines more efficiently, he would have to live in grain-growing country, and he moved to the Chicago, Illinois, area. McCormick's reaper gradually changed the face of agriculture by making grains much cheaper to harvest. McCormick's Virginia home and workshop beside Steeles Tavern near Lexington are open to the public. ■

ginia is a major producer of potatoes, peanuts, tobacco, apples, and turkeys. Winchester and Front Royal in the Piedmont are the center of the apple industry.

Farms in Virginia are not very large. They average only about 180 acres (73 ha). That is fairly typical by the standards of old eastern states. Virginia's farms bring in almost $2.5 billion a year, placing it twenty-ninth in the nation. It produces 103 million pounds (47 million kg) of tobacco, which made it sixth among the tobacco-growing states.

The Big Companies

In 1838, a railway was built that traveled the 8 miles (13 km) from Petersburg to Hopewell (called City Point at that time). The com-

Virginia Ham with Redeye Gravy

Virginia ham is a cured, smoked, and aged ham, traditionally made from hogs raised on peanuts. Ham with Redeye Gravy is a popular dish all over the South, but tastes particularly good when made with Virginia ham.

Ingredients:

4 Virginia ham steaks, 1/2-inch thick, with fat left on

1/2 cup of freshly brewed black coffee

Directions:

Fry ham steaks in their own fat in a heavy skillet until brown, about five to six minutes each side. Remove steaks from skillet and set aside on a warm platter.

Add the coffee to the grease in the skillet and stir over low heat until the gravy starts to turn brown, about five minutes. Do not allow the gravy to boil. Pour over the steaks on the platter and serve at once.

pany that built the railway is still in existence as Norfolk Southern, headquartered in Norfolk. In addition to railway-freight facilities, the company owns North American Van Lines, one of the nation's large moving companies.

Norfolk Southern is only one of the big corporations headquartered in Virginia. Mobil Corporation in Fairfax is the second-largest oil company and eighth-largest company of any kind in the United States. General Dynamics in Falls Church makes tanks and submarines.

Gannett Company of Arlington is one of the biggest publishing companies. It owns ninety-two daily newspapers, including *USA*

Mobil Corporation's headquarters

Today, which is America's largest daily. In close association with Gannett is the new Newseum, a journalism museum located in Rosslyn, the section of Arlington closest to Washington.

Another northern Virginia city, McLean, has a different flavor, with Mars, Inc. This maker of Milky Way, Snickers, and M&Ms is second only to Hershey of Pennsylvania in chocolate.

Most of Virginia's high-technology companies are located in northern Virginia. In fact, the area is second only to so-called Silicon Valley in California in its number of high-tech jobs. Loudoun County, which was open fields when Dulles International Airport was built, is now a major business area. WorldCom is planning to build a huge high-tech center there. Motorola is building a large facility near Richmond, in association with Virginia Commonwealth University. It will conduct research and carry out manufacturing of computer and other electronics parts.

What Virginia Grows, Manufactures, and Mines

Agriculture	Manufacturing	Mining
Potatoes	Chemicals	Coal
Peanuts	Tobacco products	
Milk	Food products	
Tobacco	Transportation equipment	

Richmond is also the home to the facilities of a number of large and growing companies, an industrial base away from northern Virginia. Circuit City, the chain of electronics stores, is headquartered there. The James River Corporation had long been known for such famous products as Dixie cups and Quilted Northern tissue. In 1997, it bought Wisconsin's Fort Howard Corporation. Fort James Corporation is the name of the new combined company. The headquarters is now in Illinois, although the company maintains offices in Richmond.

Richmond's Reynolds Metals, which is second after the Aluminum Company of America in the production of aluminum, was started by a relative of R. J. Reynolds, the founder of one of the biggest tobacco companies. Reynolds Metals makes the foil used in cigarette packs.

Chesapeake Bay

The bay is an important economic advantage to Virginia, though not as great as it is for Maryland. While Virginians cross the bay to reach the Eastern Shore for vacations, those Virginians who have long lived on the bay try to make a living from it.

Commercial fishers in Chesapeake Bay are called watermen. The old-timers catch crabs on trotlines, which have bait placed at intervals along the line. More recently, watermen have used crab pots. These are cubes of metallic screening into which bait is placed. The crabs can reach in to get the bait but can't get out again. The crabs that fishers catch may be hardshell (with the full shell on) or softshell (with the shell shed for molting). People who live near the bay enjoy crab boils for special occasions.

Watermen catch both fish and shellfish, but both categories are becoming endangered—as are the watermen themselves. The bay has been greatly over-fished, and its waters are polluted. Farms are plowed and planted right up to the edge of the bay. Sadly, that usually means also that the fields are doused with chemicals right up to the edge of the bay. Rain then carries the chemicals into the water.

Clamming in Chesapeake Bay

The Port Cities

Virginia's port cities were very important after the Civil War because it took several years for the railroads to be rebuilt. Virginians depended on their rivers and coasts for transportation. Norfolk became a major cotton port. Within ten years, 250,000 bales of cotton a year were being shipped abroad from Virginia.

Cotton isn't just shipped from Virginia. It is also woven there. At Danville, south of Roanoke, the Dan River was put to use powering about 1,880 textile mills. The Dan River Cotton Mills were among the largest mills in the world and still produce fine cotton textiles today.

One of the largest shipyards in the world was Newport News Shipbuilding and Dry Dock Company. Among the many ships

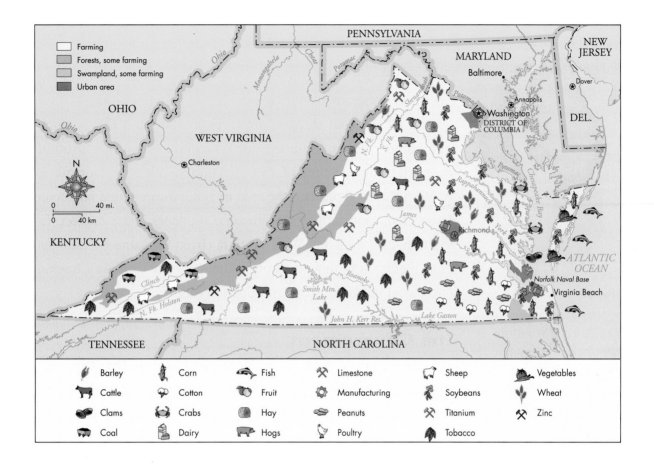

Legend (map)

- Farming
- Forests, some farming
- Swampland, some farming
- Urban area

Barley	Corn	Fish	Limestone	Sheep	Vegetables
Cattle	Cotton	Fruit	Manufacturing	Soybeans	Wheat
Clams	Crabs	Hay	Peanuts	Titanium	Zinc
Coal	Dairy	Hogs	Poultry	Tobacco	

constructed and launched there was the *United States,* the last great American passenger liner, and several huge U.S. aircraft carriers, such as the *Enterprise* and the *Forrestal.*

Gradually, Norfolk remained the only big port city in Virginia because new ships were too big to go up the rivers. Norfolk also became important nationally because it was one of the few port cities that had ample supplies of cheap coal available for refueling the new steamships.

Three major railroads carried coal from throughout the United States to the port area. Huge quantities of coal also moved from

The First Black Female Banker

Maggie Lena Walker of Richmond was America's first female bank president. Born in 1836, this African-American woman established the St. Luke Penny Savings Bank in the early 1900s. Eventually she turned her enterprise into the Consolidated Bank and Trust Company, which survived the Depression, when many larger banks failed. As she succeeded, she became an important benefactor of the black people of Richmond. ∎

Hampton Roads north and south along the coast as coal-burning electricity generators began to be built in all major cities.

Not all the coal shipped out through Hampton Roads came from other places. Southwestern Virginia, centering around Tazewell County, is noted for its coal mines. When the Norfolk & Western Railroad reached the area in 1882, the coal that had been discovered, especially at Pocahontas, suddenly had a market. In addition, coal mined in West Virginia (from the same Pocahontas Coal Fields) was moved through the state on Virginia's tracks. These coal fields are still in production today.

The Government

The federal government is the largest employer in the state. Virginians work in both government offices, especially in northern Virginia, and in the military. The Norfolk Naval Base is probably the largest in the world. The George Bush Center for Central Intelligence is located at Langley, near Washington. The Department of Defense is housed at the Pentagon in Arlington County.

NASA's Langley Research Center at Hampton is an important space and aeronautics research facility. It began in 1917 and today it has forty wind tunnels that test every aspect of aeronautics. NASA also has a launch facility for small rockets on the coast of Virginia on Wallops Island. Also located at Wallops Island are receiving stations for various international satellites.

Visitors

Hot Springs, near the West Virginia border, was founded as a resort long before Virginia, let alone West Virginia, was a state. Visitors came there in the early 1700s to soak in the hot waters that bubble up from the earth. The first hotel was built there in 1766. It is still the home of a grand old resort hotel called The Homestead.

At the other side of the state, oceanside resorts are popular throughout much of the year. Virginia Beach, the Chincoteague area on the Eastern Shore, and many smaller fine beaches draw visitors to the sea.

Millions of visitors come to the Washington, D.C., area every year, and many of those people cross the river into Virginia. They come to see the famous landmarks and enjoy the fascinating history. In other parts of the state, the incredible beaches, the historically important American Revolution and Civil War sites, as well as the beautiful mountains draw visitors. Tourism brings in almost $10 billion a year.

CHAPTER NINE

The People, Faith, and Learning

Harvesting crops by hand

The people of the South are known for their hospitality. This trait grew out of the early days in which there were no towns, only widespread plantations. Visitors were important to plantation people, and every visitor was welcome. This hospitality was extended to everyone.

The plantation owners were not just glorified farmers. In fact, the plantation system produced leaders who had considerable knowledge in many areas, including law and public administration. Among the people the system produced were the old familiar names of American history, such as Patrick Henry, George Washington, Thomas Jefferson, and James Monroe.

Because of the slavery that developed on those plantations, however, much of the last 150 years has seen white people and black people leading parallel but rarely touching lives. In the 1990 census, 77.4 percent of Virginia's 6,216,568 people were white and 18.8 percent were African-Americans.

There are only two small Native American reservations in Virginia, both belonging to Algonquin peoples. The Pamunkey people and the Mattiponi people have land on two small rivers that form the larger York River north of Richmond. The Chickahominy people (also Algonquin-speaking) tend to live in a cluster between the

Opposite: Sailboats on the Chesapeake

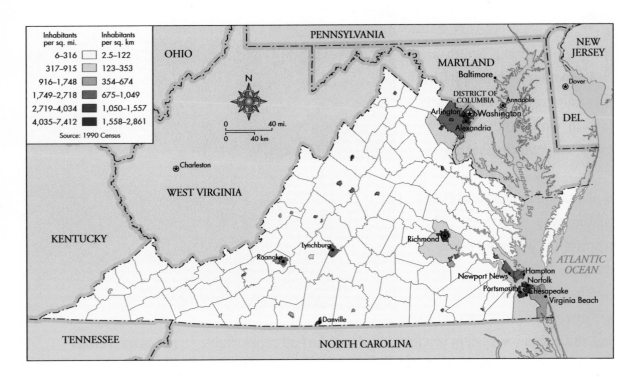

Legend:

Inhabitants per sq. mi.	Inhabitants per sq. km
6–316	2.5–122
317–915	123–353
916–1,748	354–674
1,749–2,718	675–1,049
2,719–4,034	1,050–1,557
4,035–7,412	1,558–2,861

Source: 1990 Census

Virginia's population density

James and York Rivers but do not have a reservation. The ancestors of all three of these Native American peoples were part of the Powhatan Confederation.

Religion—Black and White

The first settlers held worship services under a sail stretched between trees. When they were able, they built a church that was 60 feet (18.3 m) long.

From the beginning, Virginians were Anglicans, following the Protestant Episcopal faith they brought from England. Among the most important—and the longest lasting—of the buildings constructed during the early decades were the churches.

The Anglican Church was the official church of the colony, until the Revolution put an end to its ties with England. In addition, colonial leaders firmly believed that there should no longer be an official church and that religion should not play a role in the governing of the state.

Groups of slaves gathered together were suspect, so they were not generally allowed to have their own church. Instead, they attended church with their white master's families and sat in separate balconies. A few black congregations were formed, but they were not allowed to hold services unless a "trustworthy" white person was present to be certain they were not planning a rebellion.

After the Civil War, the most important thing the freed blacks did was build their own churches. Churches provided opportunities for friendship, economic support, and education. Richmond Theological School for Freedmen (which later became Virginia Union University) was opened within months after the end of the war.

Baptists in the South paid no attention to skin color when a person expressed an interest in joining the church. Thus, most African-American churches built in the years following the Civil War were Baptist.

Education—Black and White

In the early years, there were only a few grammar schools, usually taught by the ministers of the local churches. The very wealthy sent their sons to England to boarding school, but the girls and most boys over twelve years old received no further education.

Virginia's first college was the second to be founded in what became the United States. The founding of the College of William and Mary was approved by the king at the request of Reverend

Founding a Nation

Lott Cary was born a slave on a plantation in Charles City County. He was hired out by his master, John Bowry, to work in a Richmond tobacco warehouse. In the city, he became a Christian and taught himself to read and write. He also became a minister, and in 1821 he led a group of other freed slaves to Monrovia, where he served as a missionary. He later wrote, "I wish to go to a country where I shall be estimated by my merit, not by my complexion." In 1828, Lott Cary was killed in a gunpowder explosion while preparing to defend Liberia against an African native attack. Nineteen years later, the colony he helped found became the nation of Liberia. ■

Hampton University

James Blair, who had represented the Bishop of London in Virginia since 1689. Blair said that "Virginians have souls to save as well as Englishmen." Blair was president of the new college for the next fifty years.

The college, only the second in the colonies, was functioning by the time the colony's government was moved to Williamsburg. The teachers at the college came from England, primarily clergymen who were prepared to train colonists to become clergymen, too. They had little luck attracting men to the ministry. However, they did train new generations of leaders.

After Nat Turner's rebellion, Virginia passed a law outlawing education for slaves. It was the rare master who taught his people to read or write. It was generally only the African-American ministers—usually freedmen—who could read and write, and usually not well. In 1863, the black people found themselves emancipated with no preparation for it.

When Thomas Jefferson's university at Charlottesville was chartered by the state government in 1819, he called the campus he designed an "academical village." He also planned the curriculum that the first students followed when classes actually began in 1825. It quickly became the second largest university in the United States at that time, second only to Harvard University. The Mary

Washington College for Women merged with the University of Virginia in the 1940s.

Hampton Institute, now Hampton University, was founded in 1868 as a training school to teach freed blacks various trades so that they could establish a solid economic base for the black community. Booker T. Washington attended Hampton. The first state-funded college for blacks in the nation was Virginia State University, established in 1882 near Petersburg.

The Struggle to Change

In 1896, the U.S. Supreme Court agreed that segregation of the races in schools was legal as long as the facilities for both races were equal. In general, between 1920 and 1950, Virginia did a fairly good job of building and equipping new schools for black students. But they still had a long way to go when, in 1954, the Supreme Court ruled in four cases that segregated schools were unconstitutional. African-Americans from Virginia brought one of the cases that changed the face of education in the United States.

Virginia continued for several years to build new separate schools for both white and black students, but soon the courts forced the boards of education to integrate the schools.

Many white schools, including those in some cities such as Norfolk and Charlottesville, closed their doors rather than admit black students. White students quickly signed up to attend private schools. Many black people, recognizing that the process of change in Virginia was going to be very painful, migrated to northern states.

Spreading Education

Virginia Estelle Randolph, the daughter of former slaves, became a famed primary-school educator. During the first decade of the twentieth century, she began to spread her methods of teaching such basics as homemaking and sanitation to black children. She used these subjects as a basis for teaching reading, writing, and arithmetic. Gradually, her methods were used all over the South, and around the world, to help raise the level of education in rural schools. She established the Virginia Randolph Education Center in Henrico County. ■

In 1963, nine years after the Supreme Court's desegregation ruling, slightly more than 0.5 percent of African-American children in Virginia were attending integrated schools. Most of those were in northern Virginia or near the military bases on Hampton Roads.

Year by year, the numbers have increased. Public schools have made the changes necessary for black and white children to receive the same education. Those children are learning to work, play, and study together.

In 1995, Virginia established higher standards of education in English, math, and other subjects. The plan also calls for the test scores of students to continually improve or schools will lose their accreditation. The outcome of the plan is being watched by other states to see if they should follow the idea.

The VMI Case

Caught in the middle between valued tradition and the twenty-first century has been the Virginia Military Institute (VMI) in Lexington. In the years since it was founded in 1839, VMI has held that each cadet should be "attached to his native state, proud of her fame, and ready in every time of deepest peril to vindicate her honor or defend her rights." But at no time did the school believe that a cadet could be a female.

It took a U.S. Supreme Court decision, calling on the Fourteenth Amendment to the Constitution, to prompt VMI to change. That amendment guarantees "equal protection" to all citizens under the laws. Written after the Civil War, it forced southern states to allow black people to vote, although they found ways around that for many decades. This time, the Fourteenth Amendment was being used in a case of gender instead of race. The U.S. Supreme Court declared that the male-only policy of the Virginia Military Institute was against the Constitution. Because it is a state-supported school, receiving federal funding, it had to change.

In the past, many Virginians have preferred to live in the past, reveling in Virginia's history. Today, more Virginians are finding it preferable to live in the present. They are making their past a living part of their present and offering it to all Americans who will cherish it, too.

Population of Virginia's Major Cities (1990 census)

Virginia Beach	393,069
Norfolk	261,229
Richmond	203,056
Arlington	170,936
Newport News	170,045
Chesapeake	151,976

CHAPTER TEN

Sports, Songs, and Stories

n 1926, the Virginia legislature outlawed blacks and whites mixing at places of entertainment. Actually, such segregation had already been in effect; it just hadn't been law. One effort by blacks to compensate was the Attucks Theater in Norfolk. It was unusual in that it was owned, designed, and built by African-Ameri-

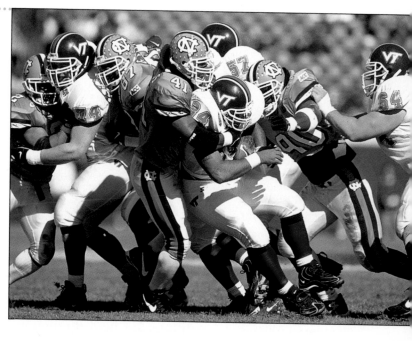

A Virginia Tech football game

cans. Named for Crispus Attucks, a black man at the Boston Massacre, it was designed by Harvey N. Johnson, a black architect. It was used for vaudeville productions and later for motion pictures.

The Team Scene

If it's professional team sports you're looking for, Virginia is not the place to find them. It's too close to Washington, D.C., with its bigger population. But business executives in northern Virginia are trying to get approval to have a Major League Baseball team. In the meantime, the Norfolk Tides minor league team is a "farm team" for the New York Mets.

There's more action at the college level. Virginia Tech (officially Virginia Polytechnic Institute and State University) at Blacksburg had a run of appearances in the football bowl games in the 1990s. In 1994, they lost to Tennessee in the Gator Bowl. The next year, they beat Texas in the Sugar Bowl and also became the National

Opposite: NASCAR driver Jeff Burton holds a trophy at Richmond's International Raceway

Invitation Tournament champions. In the 1996 Orange Bowl, Virginia Tech lost to Nebraska.

The Virginia Tech Gobblers play in the Big East Conference. The University of Virginia Cavaliers play in the Atlantic Coast Conference. The VMI Keydets play in the Southern Conference. The William and Mary Tribe play in the Atlantic Ten, along with the University of Richmond Spiders.

Taking Advantage of the Setting

Northern Virginia has long been horse country. Culpeper is an important part of the eastern horse-riding circuit. Equestrian competitions are held throughout the year. It was in Culpeper that Christopher Reeve, the film actor who had played Superman, was paralyzed in a fall in 1995.

The Virginia spas of Hot Springs and White Sulphur Springs are famous for one of their golfers, as well as for the amenities of the resorts. Famed golfer Sam Snead was born near Hot Springs and got his start playing golf at the Homestead. He also spent almost forty years as the golfing professional at the Greenbrier and won more than 80 tournaments of the Professional Golfers' Association during his career.

Stock-car racing is popular in Virginia. There are NASCAR (National Association for Stock Car Auto Racing) tracks in Richmond and Martinsville. In the Blue Ridge, where the race track follows the steep curves and hills of the mountains, some people say the sport's popularity came from the mountain folk who made their own whiskey and had to outrun the law.

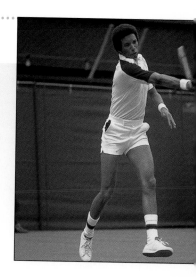

The Honorable Champ

Arthur Ashe, African-American tennis champion, was born in Richmond. He became the first black person to win the United States Tennis Open and the Wimbledon Men's Singles, both among the top tennis championships in the world.

When Ashe died in 1993, Virginia governor Douglas Wilder had his body lie in state in the Governor's Mansion. Arthur Ashe was the first person to be so honored since the death of Confederate general "Stonewall" Jackson in 1863. ■

Country Music

Country music writer and singer Patsy Cline was born Virginia Patterson Hensley in Winchester. A member of the Country Music Hall of Fame, she died in a plane crash just as her career was peaking, but her music has lived on. There is a Patsy Cline Memorial Highway in Winchester. In 1993, the U.S. Postal Service issued a Patsy Cline postage stamp.

Other country music makers include the Statler Brothers from Staunton. They are neither brothers, nor are they named Statler, but they are—and have been for many years—award-winners. These four men grew up together in Staunton in the Shenandoah Valley. They hold an annual Fourth of July "Happy Birthday U.S.A." party in their Virginia town.

A less commercial kind of country music is recognized at the Blue Ridge Institute. The institute was founded at Ferrum College in Ferrum to try to preserve the culture of the Blue Ridge people. It holds an annual Blue Ridge Folklife Festival where some of the old-time skills and crafts—including making musical instru-

Ella Fitzgerald

Pearl Bailey

ments—are exhibited. The institute was named the State Folklore Center in 1986.

Newport News was the birthplace of two of the greatest female jazz singers—Ella Fitzgerald and Pearl Bailey, both African-Americans. One of the great jazz singers of all time, Ella Fitzgerald recorded music for all the great composers and virtually invented the technique of scat singing, in which the singer sounds like a brass instrument. Pearl Bailey was an elegant woman with a mellow voice who appeared in many movies and stage shows. She also served as the U.S. goodwill ambassador to the United Nations.

Wolf Trap Farm Park for the Performing Arts, located at Vienna, is unusual in that it is an outdoor concert hall run by the National Park Service. Its center stage, in a pavilion called the Filene Center, is set among rolling hills. Its fine acoustics let people who don't otherwise get to concerts hear the National Symphony Orchestra and great soloists.

The Writers

The earliest Virginia writer was Captain John Smith, leader of Jamestown. Most of what we know of the trying years of 1607, 1608, and 1609, when the feeble colony might well have failed, comes from his amazingly descriptive books, such as *The True Travels, Adventures and Observations of Captaine John Smith in Europe, Asia, Africa and America*. Novelist Ellen Glasgow was born and died in Richmond. Her novels were acclaimed as giving a vivid picture of life in the South. Her fictional city of Queenborough was based on Richmond. Taken together, her novels have been described as presenting a realistic social history of the

Tales of the Supernatural

Edgar Allan Poe was the Boston-born author of such dark, eerie stories as "The Tell-Tale Heart" and "The Fall of the House of Usher." He was raised in Richmond by a foster family named Allan. From 1834 to 1837, he worked as editor of the *Southern* *Literary Messenger* magazine, but was fired from that job. His story "The Gold Bug" was supposedly written at Claremont Manor, the home of the Allan family. The Edgar Allan Poe Museum in Richmond contains a great deal of Poe memorabilia. ■

struggling state in the years following the Civil War. Among her many books are *Virginia, Barren Ground,* and *They Stooped to Folly.* She received a Pulitzer Prize in 1941 for her last book, *In This Our Life.*

Writer James Branch Cabell also used Richmond to create his city of Lichfield, but his stories were very different from those of Ellen Glasgow. He created a kind of fantasy world which he called Poictesme. Though his medieval fantasy world was located in France, readers could recognize it as Virginia. Cabell became a favorite of literary figures when his book *Jurgen,* published in 1919, was censored for several years.

Writer William Styron was a Newport News native. His first novel, which gained him considerable fame, was *Lie Down in Darkness.* It takes place in Virginia. He is most noted for *The Confessions of Nat Turner,* published in 1967, which tells the story of the rebellion of that Virginia slave from Turner's point of view. It won the Virginia author a Pulitzer Prize. His 1979 novel, *Sophie's Choice,* was made into a film.

William Styron

Timeline

United States History

1607 The first permanent English settlement is established in North America at Jamestown.

1620 Pilgrims found Plymouth Colony, the second permanent English settlement.

1776 America declares its independence from Britain.

1783 The Treaty of Paris officially ends the Revolutionary War in America.

1787 The U.S. Constitution is written.

Virginia State History

1584 Walter Raleigh informs Queen Elizabeth that the region around Roanoke Island is attractive. She names the area Virginia after her nickname "The Virgin Queen."

1607 The first colony of Jamestown is established.

1612 John Rolfe begins to grow tobacco in Virginia, creating income for the settlement.

1619 African slaves are first brought to Jamestown by the Dutch. The House of Burgesses in Virginia is established.

1622 Powhatan Indians attack white settlers at Jamestown. English settlers there are spurred into eliminating Native Americans from Virginia lands.

1676 Nathaniel Bacon and supporters rebel against the government.

1775 George Washington is chosen as commander in chief of the Continental Army.

1776 The Declaration of Independence is written by Virginian Thomas Jefferson. The Virginia Declaration of Rights, which served as the model for the Constitution's Bill of Rights, is introduced by George Mason.

1780 The British army enters Virginia through its mountains and the Carolinas.

1781 British general Cornwallis surrenders to Washington's army near Yorktown, essentially ending the American Revolution.

1788 Virginia ratifies the Constitution, becoming the tenth state on June 25.

United States History

Louisiana Purchase almost doubles **1803**
the size of the United States.

United States and Britain **1812-15**
fight the War of 1812.

The North and South fight **1861-65**
each other in the American Civil War.

The United States is **1917-18**
involved in World War I.

Stock market crashes, **1929**
plunging the United States into
the Great Depression.

The United States **1941-45**
fights in World War II.
The United States becomes a **1945**
charter member of the U.N.

The United States **1951-53**
fights in the Korean War.

The U.S. Congress enacts a series of **1964**
groundbreaking civil rights laws.

The United States **1964-73**
engages in the Vietnam War.

The United States and other **1991**
nations fight the brief
Persian Gulf War against Iraq.

Virginia State History

1789 George Washington is elected first
president of the United States.

1831 Nat Turner leads revolts in Virginia.

1861 Virginia secedes from the Union,
joining the South in the American
Civil War. The Battle of Bull Run,
the first major Civil War battle, is
fought in Virginia.

1863 West Virginia is formed from northwestern Virginia counties.

1865 Robert E. Lee surrenders at Appomattox, ending the American Civil War.

1870 Virginia rejoins the Union.

1912 Woodrow Wilson, a native Virginian, is
elected president of the United States.

1959 Integration of public schools takes
place in Virginia.

1990 L. Douglas Wilder of Virginia becomes
the first African-American governor in
the United States.

Fast Facts

Monument Avenue, Richmond

Statehood date	June 25,1788, the 10th state
Origin of state name	In honor of Queen Elizabeth, the so-called "Virgin Queen" of England
State capital	Richmond
State nickname	Old Dominion, Mother of Presidents
State bird	Cardinal
State flower and tree	Flowering dogwood
State dog	American foxhound
State fish	Brook trout
State fossil	*Chesapecten jeffersonius*
State shell	Oyster
State insect	Tiger swallowtail butterfly
State song	None
State folk dance	Square dance
State boat	Chesapeake Bay deadrise
State beverage	Milk
State fair	Late September or early October at Richmond
Total area; rank	42,326 sq. mi. (109,625 sq km); 35th

Flowering dogwood

Lake Gaston

Land; rank	39,598 sq. mi. (102,559 sq km); 37th
Water; rank	2,728 sq. mi. (7,066 sq km); 15th
Inland water; **rank**	1,000 sq. mi. (2,590 sq km); 22nd
Coastal water; **rank**	1,728 sq. mi. (4,476 sq km); 5th
Geographic center	Southwest of Buckingham, 5 miles (8 km)
Latitude and longitude	Virginia is located approximately between 36° 32' and 39° 27' N and 75° 15' and 83° 41' W
Highest point	Mount Rogers, 5,729 feet (1,746 m)
Lowest point	Sea level at the Atlantic Ocean
Largest city	Virginia Beach
Number of counties	95, plus 40 independent cities
Population; rank	6,216,568 (1990 census); 12th
Density	153 persons per sq. mi. (59 per sq km)
Population distribution	69% urban, 31% rural

Ethnic distribution (does not equal 100%)

White	77.44%
African-American	18.80%
Hispanic	2.59%
Asian and Pacific Islanders	2.57%
Other	0.94%
Native American	0.25%

Record high temperature	110°F (43°C) at Columbia on July 5, 1900, and at Balcony Falls on July 15, 1954
Record low temperature	–30°F (–34°C) at Mountain Lake on January 22, 1985
Average July temperature	75°F (24°C)

Virginia Beach

Richmond National
Battlefield Park

**Average January
temperature** 36°F (2°C)

**Average annual
precipitation** 43 inches (109 cm)

Natural Areas and Historic Sites

National Park
Shenandoah National Park in the Blue Ridge Mountains has the famous Shenandoah River running through it. Most spectacular are the colors of the trees in autumn.

National Battlefield Park
Manassas commemorates the Battles of First and Second Manassas, also known as Bull Run. Here, Confederate Brigadier General Thomas Jackson was given his nickname "Stonewall."

Petersburg National Battlefield is the site where Northern general Ulysses S. Grant cut off the supplies to Southern general Robert E. Lee, forcing him to evacuate his troops. It includes the Battle of the Crater site.

Richmond honors the site of eleven battlefields from the American Civil War, including Cold Harbor and Malvern Hill. It was established in 1936.

National Historic Site
Maggie L. Walker honors the first woman to start a bank and to serve as a bank president in the United States. The African-American woman lived on the site for thirty years.

National Historical Park
Appomattox Court House is the place where Confederate General Robert E. Lee surrendered, marking the end of the American Civil War. Guests can walk 6 miles (10 km) along the History Trail and see the McLean home, where Lee formally surrendered.

Shenandoah National
Park

Cumberland Gap

Colonial on the Lower Peninsula includes the land of the first English settlement at Jamestown and the site of the last American Revolution battle, at Yorktown. The Henry Memorial Cross marks the place where the settlers first landed in 1607.

Cumberland Gap is a large gap in the Cumberland Mountains. Through the Gap, Native Americans, settlers, and animals forged their way west.

National Memorials and Monuments

Arlington House, or the *Robert E. Lee Memorial*, in McLean is a tribute to the Southern general of the American Civil War. Lee lived in the house for thirty years.

Booker T. Washington National Monument is the 207-acre (84-ha) tobacco farm on which the famous humanitarian and educator was born into slavery.

George Washington Birthplace National Monument has buildings dating back to the eighteenth century with more than 16,000 artifacts from Washington's history.

National Military Park

Fredericksburg and Spotsylvania is the largest military park in the world, sitting on almost 9,000 acres (3,645 ha). It honors the men who fought in four battles on the site and contains the "Stonewall" Jackson Shrine.

National Seashore

Assateague Island covers 18,000 acres (7,000 ha) in the states of Virginia and Maryland. Especially breathtaking are the Assateague wild ponies that roam the shoreline.

State Parks

False Cape, south of Sandbridge and southeast of Virginia Beach, is renowned for its isolation—visitors must hike or bike 5 miles (8 km) to get to it. A wonder of nature, False Cape has sandy beaches, marshlands, and a maritime forest.

Iwo Jima Memorial

Grayson Highlands between Damascus and Independence is bordered by Virginia's two highest mountains. Visitors will enjoy seeing the Jones Homestead, with its log cabin, spring house, cane mill, and cemetery.

At *Douthat,* north of Clifton Forge, outdoor lovers can take a paddleboat tour of Douthat Lake and see the many buildings constructed by the Civilian Conservation Corps.

Sports Teams

NCAA Teams (Division 1)

College of William and Mary Tribe
George Mason University Patriots
Hampton University Pirates
James Madison University Duke
Liberty University Flames
Old Dominion University Monarchs
Radford University Highlanders
University of Virginia Cavaliers
Virginia Commonwealth University Rams
Virginia Military Institute Keydets
Virginia Polytechnic Institute & State University Gobblers/ Hokies

Cultural Institutions

Libraries

The *Jefferson–Madison Regional Library* (main branch in Charlottesville) provides service to the city of Charlottesville, Thomas Jefferson's home county of Albemarle, and three more counties. This public library was founded from the private libraries of Jefferson, James Monroe, and other Virginians.

The *Library of Virginia* (Richmond) was built in 1823 and has a vast collection of materials on Virginia's history. The library also sponsors many events and exhibitions relating to Virginia.

A Virginia Tech game

Hampton University

College of William and Mary

Museums

At the *Frontier Culture Museum of Virginia* (Staunton), visitors can see re-creations of European life before immigrants came to America as well as their life in America. Authentic farms from Europe and an early American farm are on the site.

The *Mariners' Museum* (Newport News) has a large display of more than 35,000 items based on ships and sailing, including ship models, paintings, and working steam engines. There is also a research library and archives.

The *Virginia Museum of Natural History* (Martinsville) has many collections of life ranging from Virginia's prehistoric years to the present day. It also has a new collection of 11 million insects from Virginia, which the Smithsonian Institution donated.

Performing Arts

Virginia has two opera companies, two symphony orchestras, and one dance company.

Universities and Colleges

In the mid-1990s, Virginia had 39 public and 50 private institutions of higher learning.

Annual Events

January–March

Highland County Maple Sugar Festival in Monterey (March)

Garden Symposium in Williamsburg (late March or early April)

April–June

International Azalea Festival in Norfolk (late April)

Dogwood Festival in Charlottesville (late April)

Shenandoah Apple Blossom Festival in Winchester (early May)

Jamestown Landing Day in Williamsburg (May)

Harborfest in Norfolk (early June)

Old Town, Alexandria

Boardwalk Art Show in Virginia Beach (late June)

Hampton Jazz Festival (late June)

July–September

Scottish Games and Gathering of the Clans in Alexandria (July)

The Big Gig in Richmond (July)

Annual Statler Brothers Independence Day celebration in Staunton (July)

Highlands Arts and Crafts Festival in Abingdon (first two weeks in August)

Old Fiddlers' Convention in Galax (August)

Neptune Festival in Virginia Beach (late September)

October–December

Danville Harvest Jubilee (October)

Oyster Festival on Chincoteague Island (October)

Olde Towne Ghost Walk in Portsmouth (late October)

Blue Ridge Folklife Festival in Ferrum (fourth Saturday in October)

The Grand Illumination in Williamsburg (early December)

Famous People

William Styron

Elizabeth Peratrovich (1911–1958)	Civil rights activist
Stephen Fuller Austin (1793–1836)	Colonizer and political leader
Pearl Bailey (1918–1990)	Jazz singer
Richard Evelyn Byrd (1888–1957)	Naval officer and polar explorer
Willa Sibert Cather (1873–1947)	Author
George Rogers Clark (1752–1818)	Frontier leader and soldier
William Clark (1770–1838)	Soldier and explorer
Henry Clay (1777–1852)	Political leader

Ella Fitzgerald (1917–1996)	Jazz singer
William Henry Harrison (1773–1841)	U.S. president
Thomas Jefferson (1743–1826)	U.S. president
Henry (Light-Horse Harry) Lee (1756–1818)	Soldier and public official
Robert E. Lee (1807–1870)	Confederate general
Meriwether Lewis (1774–1809)	Soldier and explorer and public official
James Madison (1751–1836)	U.S. president
John Marshall (1755–1835)	Chief justice of the United States
Cyrus Hall McCormick (1809–1884)	Inventor and industrialist
James Monroe (1758–1831)	U.S. president
Pocahontas (1595?–1617)	Native American figure
Edgar Allan Poe (1809–1849)	Author
Powhatan (1550?–1618)	Native American leader
Walter Reed (1851–1902)	Physician
George Campbell Scott (1927–)	Actor
William Clark Styron Jr. (1925–)	Author
Zachary Taylor (1784–1850)	Soldier and U.S. president
John Tyler (1790–1862)	U.S. president
Booker Taliaferro Washington (1856–1915)	Educator
George Washington (1732–1799)	Soldier and U. S. president
Thomas Woodrow Wilson (1856–1924)	Educator and U.S. president

Thomas Woodrow Wilson

To Find Out More

History

- Cooke, William. *A Historical Album of Virginia*. Brookfield, Conn.: Millbrook Press, 1995.

- Fradin, Dennis Brindell. *Virginia*. Chicago: Childrens Press, 1992.

- Fradin, Dennis Brindell. *The Virginia Colony*. Chicago: Childrens Press, 1986.

- Richards, Norman. *Monticello*. Danbury, Conn.: Children's Press, 1995.

- Sakurai, Gail. *The Jamestown Colony*. Danbury, Conn.: Children's Press, 1997.

- Sirvaitis, Karen. *Virginia*. Minneapolis: Lerner Publications Company, 1991.

- Thompson, Kathleen. *Virginia*. Austin, Tex.: Raintree/Steck Vaughn, 1996.

Biographies

- Cannon, Marian G. *Robert E. Lee*. New York: Franklin Watts, Inc., 1993.

- Davidson, Mary R. *Dolly Madison: Famous First Lady*. Illus. by Erica Merkling. Broomall, Penn.: Chelsea House Publishers, 1992.

- Gross, Ruth Belov. *If You Grew Up With George Washington*. Illus. by Emily Arnold McCully. New York: Scholastic, 1993.

- Kliment, Bud. *Ella Fitzgerald*. Broomall, Penn.: Chelsea House Publishers, 1989.

- Levert, Suzanne. *Edgar Allan Poe*. Broomall, Penn.: Chelsea House Publishers, 1992.

Old, Wendie C. *Thomas Jefferson*. Springfield, N.J.: Enslow Publishers, Inc., 1997.

Websites

■ **State of Virginia**
http://www.state.va.us
The official state website for Virginia

■ **Virginia Historical Society**
http://www.vahistorical.org
For information on services and history of the museum of state history for Virginia

■ **Virtual Library of Virginia**
http://www.viva.lib.va.us
A group of academic libraries that provide electronic images, journals, books, and other materials.

Addresses

■ **Office of the Governor**
State Capitol, 3rd Floor
Richmond, VA 23219
For information on the government of the Commonwealth of Virginia

■ **Virginia Department of Historic Resources**
2801 Kensington Avenue
Richmond, VA 23221
For information about architectural and archaeo-logical sites in Virginia

■ **Gunston Hall Plantation**
Mason Neck, VA 22079
A national landmark, this is the home of the well-respected George Mason, who wrote the Virginia Bill of Rights and helped create the U.S. government.

Index

Page numbers in *italics* indicate illustrations.

Meet the
Author

Jean Blashfield lived in northern Virginia for several years while working in Washington, D.C., and became fascinated by the ever-present history of the state and its people. She made many trips throughout the state, delighting in the amazing variety of scenery, from ocean to mountains, and the intriguing stories people told.

During many years in publishing, Blashfield developed several encyclopedias, including the classic *Young People's Science Encyclopedia* for Children's Press. While living in Arlington, Virginia, she opened offices for Funk & Wagnalls to create a general encyclopedia for young students.

In addition to living in Virginia, she has lived and worked in Chicago; London, England; and Washington, D.C. But when she married Wallace Black (a Chicago publisher, writer, and pilot), they moved to Wisconsin. Today, she has two college-age children, three cats, and two computers in her Victorian home in Delavan, Wisconsin.

Jean Blashfield has written about eighty books, most of them for young people. She likes best to write about interesting places, but she loves history and science, too. In fact, one of her big advantages as a writer is that she becomes fascinated by just about every subject she investigates. She has created an encyclopedia of aviation and space, written popular books on murderers and house plants, and had a lot of fun creating an early book on the things women have done, called *Hellraisers, Heroines, and Holy Women.*

She and Wally later formed their own company, which took advantage of Jean's massive collection of 3 x 5 cards. The cards contained interesting tidbits of information about many states, their places and people. Today, she has all that research on computer. In fact, she uses computers to broaden her research on Virginia and many other subjects.She has become an avid Internet surfer and is working on her own website, but she'll never give up her trips to the library.

She has written several America the Beautiful books for Children's Press and has been particularly pleased to be able to write this book, on the state where the nation began.

Photo Credits

Photographs ©:

AllSport USA: 123 (Tony Duffy), 120, 121, 132 (Craig Jones)

Archive Photos: 11, 19, 49, 135

Art Resource, NY: 9 (Erich Lessing), 29, 36 bottom right (National Portrait Gallery, Smithsonian Institution)

Brown Brothers: 34

Corbis-Bettmann: 118 (UPI), 26 bottom, 28 top, 32, 36 top, 36 bottom left, 43, 44, 86, 125 right

Dennis Brack: 6 top center, 72, 134 top

Envision: 105 (Steven Needham)

Gamma-Liaison, Inc.: 75, 131 bottom (Ron Alston), 124 bottom (Cynthia Johnson), 125 left, 134 bottom (Dominique Nabakov), 46 (NASA), 124 top (Kip Rano), 6 top left, 57, 71 (Wolfgang Käehler)

Jay Mallin: 106

National Geographic Image Collection: 13 (Robert Maddenngs), 56 (Jay Mallin), cover, back cover, 85, 100, 112 (Medford Taylor)

North Wind Picture Archives: 14, 17, 18, 22, 23, 26 top, 30, 31, 38, 42, 66, 101, 102, 104

Photo Researchers: 93, 133 bottom

(Margot Granitsas), 81, 82 (Mary Ann Hemphill), 7 bottom, 91 (John Kaprielian), 6 bottom, 63 (Michael Lustbader), 61, 131 top (Kenneth Murray), 103 (Bruce Roberts), 90 top (Gregory K. Scott), 83 (Don Carl Steffen)

Photri: 7 top right, 108 (E. Drifmeyer), 54, 129 top (B. Howe), 89, 90 bottom, 128 top, 128 bottom (Everett C. Johnson), 76 (Jim Kirby), 7 top left, 80, 129 bottom (B. Kulik), 7 top center, 99

Stock Montage, Inc.: 20, 28 bottom, 33, 35, 41, 45, 50, 64

The Library of Virginia: 16, 24, 47, 48, 95, 110, 113

Tom Stack & Associates: 70 (Terry Donnelly)

Tony Stone Images: 73 (Rob Boudreau), 88 (Cathlyn Melloan), 8 (David Muench)

Virginia Tourism Corporation: 6 top right, 59 (Nancy Hoyt Belcher)

Visuals Unlimited: 67 (Gary W. Carter), 12 (Rob Simpson), 2, 130 bottom (Rob & Ann Simpson)

Words and Pictures: 52, 55, 98, 116, 130 top, 133 top (Carl and Ann Purcell)

Maps by XNR Productions, Inc.